What others are saying about *Facing A Crowd:*

"**An entertaining and informative guide** to help you stand tall and push through one of your biggest fears...facing an audience. I highly recommend it."

> Susan Jeffers, Ph.D., — Author of *Feel the Fear and Do It Anyway* and *Feel the Fear and Beyond*

"**Great book!** Very useful information for anyone who may ever have to speak to a group of people. As a young woman in the early 1970s, one skill allowed me to break into the "man's world" of professional commercial sales - confidence and poise speaking to small groups and large. This book can help anyone gain confidence and reach higher personal or professional goals."

> Jean Russell Nave — Motivational speaker, retired

"**The author** shares the inside details and practical information that only someone who has been there could know. *Facing a Crowd* is **fascinating reading for speakers at all levels.**"

> Dan Poynter — Publisher, speaker, and author of *The Self-Publishing Manual*

"**A *must- read*** for anyone wanting to communicate more effectively - whether at staff meetings, board meetings or presentations to hundreds. Wonderful format and written with great style and humor. This book will help you achieve your full potential in public speaking."

> Barbara Merlin — Manpower Development Specialist

"**Exquisitely presented, punctuated with humor, and fun to read!** Finally, a hands-on book that is easy to comprehend. Whether your goal is to overcome slight apprehension or manage downright paralyzing fear – this book is for you. Clinton provides clever tools and strategies you can use today to enhance your skills dramatically, become a more polished speaker, and relax! I cannot think of a single client or associate - whether college professor, student, CEO or small business owner – who would not benefit from the many strong pointers that are provided on every page."

> Ann Golden Egle, — CPCC, Motivational Coach, speaker and writer

FACING A CROWD

How to foil your fear
of public speaking

by

Keith Clinton

DRAKE PUBLISHING
BEND, OREGON

Facing A Crowd
How to foil your fear of public speaking
Copyright © 2002 by Keith Clinton

Published by:

DRAKE PUBLISHING
P.O. Box 8524
Bend, Oregon 97708-8524
www.drakepublishing.biz

Printed by Central Plains Book Manufacturing   Winfield, Kansas
on acid free paper.

05 04 03 02   10 9 8 7 6 5 4 3 2 1

Disclaimer:

Publisher's Cataloging-in-Publication
 (Provided by Quality Books, Inc.)

Clinton, Keith.
    Facing a crowd : how to foil your fear of public
speaking / by Keith Clinton. – 1st ed.
    p. cm.
    Includes bibliographical references and index.
    LCCN 2002090006
    ISBN 0-9709919-6-7
    1. Public speaking. 2. Speech anxiety. I. Title.

PN4121.C55 2002   808.5'1
                       QBI02-200181

Acknowledgements

So many people helped in the development of this book - rather than risk leaving someone out of a lengthy list, let me just say thank you, thank you one and all! We both know who you are, and unless I messed up badly, you already have a copy of this in your hands.

My deepest appreciation goes out to the following few who deserve special recognition:

- My wife Jeannie – Thank you for your intelligent ideas, fathomless faith, and unparalleled patience.
- Graphic designer/Illustrator Traci Mc. Merritt – You're top-notch! I can't thank you enough for your hard work.
- Photographer David Morris – Thanks for the great shots. You were very patient with me and my rowdy crowd.
- Editor Diane Dean – What an eye for detail! I wish I had paid closer attention to my English teachers, and I know you wish I had too.
- Illustrator Abigail Clinton – My beautiful daughter finding her way in sunny CA. Terrific concepts!
- Staff and members of the Publishers Marketing Association for their expert advice.
- Bend Senior High School for the use of their auditorium.

This book is a compilation of much of the wisdom that I have garnered over the years regarding public speaking. Having read stacks of books, scores of web sites, and listened to so many of my fellow Toastmasters and others speak on the subject (prior to ever having the notion of writing a book) I cannot tell you the exact origin of much of the material found herein. Some of it came from little scraps of paper on which I had jotted down notes over the years. Most of it however was simply retrieved from the memory banks of my gray matter and put down on paper for the edification of interested parties such as yourself.

Credit has been given with quotation marks and/or bibliographic references for every source of which I have definite knowledge of its origin. I dearly thank the originators of those works. I trust their words and stories in this educational text will inspire you as much as they did me. And I encourage and recommend that you seek out those original works. They are worth it.

Dedicated to...

My wife Jeannie, a rock of encouragement;

My inspirational children and friends; and

Tom Felando, an affable, energetic coworker, born the same year as myself. Tom's sudden death, while playing volleyball, reminded me that our time in this dimension is finite and that things we want to accomplish must be worked on today, not some day.

SUCCESS...

It is not a destination

we'll arrive at some day,

But what we do

along the way.

Contents

Part III   TO PREPARE QUALITY PRESENTATIONS...

Part IV   TO ACHIEVE YOUR SPEAKING GOALS...

Still can't speak?

Final thoughts and a request

Appendix

Preface

I have been where perhaps you are today. For over thirty years I feared public speaking. Just the *thought* of getting up in front of people, even to simply introduce myself, made my heart race, my face flush, and my knees quiver. I kept this problem to myself though and simply tried to avoid ever being the center of attention.

Because of my fear I held myself back, didn't join in, didn't go after the career I really wanted and in many ways squandered the dreams of my youth. But I finally grew tired of living like this, and I became angry with myself for not accomplishing what I knew I was capable of both personally and professionally. So I set out to change.

For months I haunted libraries and bookstores, reading every book and magazine I could find which dealt with fear, shyness, phobias, stage fright, and public speaking. I even read dozens of biographies of professional entertainers to see how they were able to do what they do so well. Slowly I discovered that my fears were not unique and my situation not hopeless. Through my research I unearthed many secrets of how we can overcome our natural fear of public expression and excel as public speakers. I then put into practice what I had learned with fantastic results.

As if a giant weight were lifted from me, I am now able to do things I could only dream about before. I have not only learned how to speak up, but also how to take control of my life. I now care a lot less about what other people think of me, than what I think of myself. I have become involved in my community, pursued my dreams of acting and singing, developed many new and fulfilling relationships with people, and have taken on jobs which required a tremendous amount of public relations and media work.

The benefits I have enjoyed in the last few years have been so profound that I felt absolutely *compelled* to write this book. I want to share what I have learned and been able to put into practice with those who may be struggling with some of the same issues that affected me for so many years.

Knowledge is power. To give *you* the power, I have boiled this book down to what I feel is the most important "how-to" information available on the subject of public speaking. Throughout these pages are proven techniques, helpful hints, quotable quotes, valuable nuggets, and useful references to other books and materials. By putting this information to work, you will be able to understand and overcome your natural fear of public speaking. Then, with practice, you will acquire the ability to face any audience, large or small, and speak confidently and skillfully.

It is my sincere hope that your newfound communication skills will bring you great joy and success in all of your personal and professional endeavors. Walter Anderson once wrote,

"Nothing diminishes anxiety faster than action."
So, let's get started.   KC

Mic the microphone

Part One

TO EASE YOUR ANXIETY...

— Chapter 1 —

Learn why public speaking is an essential skill

◆◆

"There are four ways, and only four ways,
in which we have contact with the world.
We are evaluated and classified
by these four contacts:
what we do, how we look,
what we say, and how we say it."

— Dale Carnegie

PUBLIC ADDRESS, SPEECH, ORAL PRESENTATION

Whatever you wish to call it, you may be surprised to learn that *most* people fear it. That's right! The vast majority of humans fear the front of the class, fear being the center of attention, and fear expressing themselves publicly. So if *you* are fearful of any of these things, stop beating yourself up. You are in extremely good company and are certifiably normal!

The excess nervousness we feel before getting up in front of a group of people is often referred to as stage fright. It is an overpowering fear that can make voices quiver and knees shake. For many of us it is devastating in that it can hold us back from ever speaking in front of more than one or two people at a time. But anyone, including you, can overcome this fear.

With this book, you will gain the knowledge and skills necessary to move beyond your anxiety. You will learn how to prepare for an oral presentation, and you will learn proven techniques and tricks-of-the-trade used by successful public speakers everywhere.

As you begin putting this information into practice, you are going to discover within yourself the confidence to proudly stand before any audience and unabashedly share your thoughts and ideas. This may be hard for you to believe right now, but it is absolutely true.

As you read this book remember one thing: Orators are not born - they are made.

Why is it important to know how to speak in front of others? Here are a few reasons:

- Gain respect.
- Get promoted.
- Make a better income.
- Begin a new career.
- Start a business.
- Be more popular.
- Feel better about yourself.
- Participate in community or club activities.
- Run for an elected office.
- Take on a leadership role.
- Do something you have always feared.

EXERCISE

Why is it important for you personally to learn how to speak well in front of groups? How would you complete the following sentence?

I want to improve my public speaking skills so I can...

Let's face it, learning to speak up and say what is on your mind is a very powerful skill to cultivate, and we all need to learn how to do it if we want to be successful.

Think for a moment about all of the chances you have had to express yourself publicly in the last several years—perhaps by making a brief statement, answering or asking a question, or giving a presentation of some kind. These opportunities may have been at your place of work in a variety of meetings, training sessions, or seminars. Or they could have come at club meetings, church gatherings, reunions, hearings, classrooms or innumerable other places.

Wherever the chance arose, did you speak up each time you had something to say? Did you make it known to the group every time you had a good solution for a problem? Did you voice your disagreement when others introduced obviously hare-brained ideas you knew could not possibly work?

Or, have you typically stayed silent, hung back, and let others do the talking? Then later, have you kicked yourself for not speaking up when you had the chance? If so, don't feel alone. In fact, so many of us do this, it is the norm rather than the exception.

By not asserting yourself and voicing your opinions, it is likely that many of the people who surround you on a daily basis really don't know who you are. The impression the world has of you may be totally different from what you are truly like inside—simply because you seldom open up and speak your mind. Because of this, your intelligence, skills, and abilities are probably being under-utilized, for people just do not know the *real* you and the tremendous wealth of ideas you have.

It is a fact that if we do not voice our thoughts and opinions in public settings, there are many people who will never get to know us. And if people don't know us, they are going to be less apt to support us, hire us, promote us, buy things from us, or vote for us. In other words, success is going to be hard to come by if we do not learn to open up and communicate with those around us.

Obviously, a great deal of interpersonal communication takes place in public settings. With this in mind, ponder for a moment how many more public meetings or gatherings you are likely to attend over the remainder of your lifetime. Think of all the people you are going to meet at such gatherings, and imagine how much better you will be able to communicate with everyone once you possess the skills and confidence to stand up and talk in front of them.

Whenever and wherever we are with people, be it one or one hundred, we are constantly given the chance to express ourselves, say what we think, and state our opinions. Because we are social beings, what we do with these opportunities really defines in large measure who we are and what we are capable of.

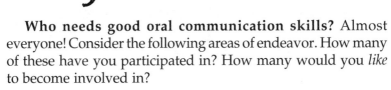

The capacity to "stand and deliver" in front of an audience often separates those who get what they want out of life from those who do not. Therefore, we simply must take advantage of chances we are given to communicate, especially in group settings. In doing so, we can pursue our dreams, show others our capabilities, positively influence people, and make meaningful changes to our world.

Who needs good oral communication skills? Almost everyone! Consider the following areas of endeavor. How many of these have you participated in? How many would you *like* to become involved in?

Education – Teachers, instructors and professors, to be effective, must engage students in an interesting and informative style. For students to get the most out of school, they need to be involved, speak up, answer questions, and ask questions when facts or concepts are unclear.

Community Service – To have a *community* there needs to be *communi*cation; whether it is among a student body, neighborhood, company, club, city, state, or nation. In order to have a sense of belonging to any organization or geographic area, people have to talk to each other one-on-one and in groups.

Commerce – The health of an economy is dependent upon the sharing of ideas and facts by entrepreneurs, board members, CEOs, executives, frontline supervisors, sales staff, and workers at all levels.

Self-employment – Being your own boss can be very rewarding. However, it means there is no one else up the line to take responsibility for making presentations to banks or other potential backers, to clients, to city councils or chambers of commerce, to employees and dozens of other potential audiences who are essential to the success of your business.

Government – Whether or not we like politics and government, elections and recounts, we need people to represent us at local, state and national levels. These people must be able to reach out and ask constituents what they think and what they want. Representatives must then be able to communicate with other representatives, then debate, negotiate, and compromise in order to write, pass, and administer the laws of the land.

News Media – Television, radio, newspapers, and magazine reporters all provide a valuable service to our modern world, which demands instantaneous and in-depth information about what is going on and why.

Religion – Religious values, morals, and traditions are preserved and passed on largely through the spoken word. Many voices are needed to effectively sustain doctrines of faith.

Entertainment – Life would certainly be dull if we did not have people who were willing to go in front of others and express themselves through music, dance, acting, poetry, comedy, magic, and more. Can you imagine what it would it be like in a world devoid of performing artists? There would be no live theater or stage productions, no story tellers, no concerts, movies, television, radio programs, or recordings of any kind. Entertainers fill what would otherwise be a huge void in our lives.

Diplomacy – Maintaining peace and a balance of power and trade in a precarious and sometimes hostile world requires people who can effectively communicate, negotiate and lead on an international scale.

Military – When peaceful, diplomatic talks fail, it is sometimes necessary to use force against aggressors. To minimize chaos, whether in times of peace or war, good communication throughout the chain of command is essential. One reason General Dwight D. Eisenhower was chosen (and successful) as the European Supreme Allied Commander in World War II was because he was an excellent communicator with a reputation for bringing people of differing viewpoints together and getting them to work toward common goals.

So why is it important for you personally to be able to express yourself in public? What is it you want to do? What do you want to accomplish?

These are questions only you can answer. But if you want anything badly enough and are ready to put your self-esteem on the line to get it, there will be no stopping you!

— Chapter 2 —

Discover the reasons behind the fear

♦♦

"I wish I didn't get so nervous."
"I'd rather die than go up there!"
"Am I the only one who feels like this?"

— Secret thoughts of millions
of people each day

It has been estimated from surveys that 85 percent of Americans experience anxiety about public speaking. [1] Eighty five percent! Just imagine how many unspoken thoughts that equates to each day. Many people (30+ percent) indicate that speaking in front of an audience is their worst fear over all others, including **death!**

When faced with a situation where we need to speak up in public, our pragmatic side may tell us, "There really is nothing to worry about. People are just people. We all have similar fears and foibles. Talking in front of this group shouldn't be any big deal, right?" Yes, but.....

Imagine this: You have been asked to give a fifteen minute presentation to a gathering of two hundred people, and you are now sitting with a few other people at the head table in a large meeting hall. The Master of Ceremonies has just concluded a few opening remarks and is now introducing you as the next speaker. You stand and walk across the raised platform to the sound of applause. At the lectern you adjust the microphone and all eyes are now focused on you. The crowd silently anticipates your first words.

Hmmm. Suddenly your pragmatic side is nowhere in sight! It just took the last bus out of town with all your baggage, leaving you standing there lost and alone facing an expectant audience. What would that be like?

EXERCISE

Take a few moments and put yourself in front of that imaginary audience of two hundred. Pay particular attention to exactly what it is that bothers you in this scene. Go ahead. Close your eyes and imagine being at the front of that meeting hall.

How did it feel? Did you experience fear? If so, what do you think caused it? Was it any of these thoughts perhaps?

People staring - All those eyes focused on you.

Making a mistake - Who would want to mess up in front of *that* many people?

Forgetting what to say - Yikes! That could be embarrassing.

Disappointing superiors - What if the boss or your parents see you make a mistake?

Looking foolish - What if no one laughs at your jokes? Or you drop your notes and then they laugh? Or worse, what if your zipper is down or blouse comes unbuttoned?!!

You may be semi-relieved to know that these are all common responses of those who are bothered by public speaking. Other feelings shared by many of us include the idea that our personal thoughts are not valid, as we sometimes have the mistaken impression that everyone else is somehow smarter than we are. This can lead us to feel that we are not worthy of being listened to. In turn, this can cause concern that if we speak up we will be wasting people's time and taking opportunities away from others whose ideas and opinions are better than ours. Oftentimes we are embarrassed at being the center of attention, but don't really know why. And occasionally we are worried that what we say will somehow offend other people.

The core of much of our self-doubt seems to center around deeper feelings such as the fear of being judged or a fear of rejection. For many, one of the most frustrating things about public speaking anxiety is that we really do not know why we are afflicted with it; we just know that we are. So let's look at some of the suggested reasons experts have put forth. Hopefully this will provide you new insight as to why you fear facing a crowd of people.

Genetics

Humans are pre-programmed with the ability to react very quickly. If startled by a loud noise, we jump. If we accidentally touch a hot stove, we pull away. If falling, we instinctively catch ourselves. We do not have to think about these reactions any more than breathing. The same is true of our physical responses to stress or external threats.

Eons ago the stress of daily life for our ancestors was different than it is today. Back then, two primary daily concerns for us would have been finding enough to eat, and making sure we were not eaten. To accomplish both of these required an instantaneous response system to help us immediately determine if something was potential food and/or a threat to our well-being. We would then at once have to size it up as to whether we could handle it and quickly either chase it with a sharp stick before it got away or sprint for the nearest tree before it got us. The marvelous mechanism allowing these split second life or death decisions and actions has been aptly named "fight or flight." Although our world has changed much since our ancestors lived in caves, we retain this same stress-response system.

How does it work? In brief, when something trips our trigger, be it a lion strolling into the cave, or a driver cutting us off at a freeway on-ramp, our endocrine system dumps strong hormones, such as adrenalin, directly into our blood stream. These hormones instantly set in motion a firestorm of activity in our bodies. Our heart rate goes up, blood pressure increases, airways dilate, and respiration rate increases. Blood flow is decreased to extremities, the digestive system, and other nonessential organs. At the same time blood flow is *increased* to the brain, heart and skeletal muscles. Glucose is dumped into the blood stream, pupils dilate, alertness increases, a feeling of urgency sweeps over us, and nerve endings stimulate the adrenal gland to reinforce and prolong all of these stress responses. Whew! That is a lot going on in the space of about one second.

So what does this all mean for you as a potential speaker? It means that many symptoms may occur as you prepare to face an audience - pounding pulse, rapid breathing, cold hands, queasy stomach, tremors, darting eyes, and a feeling that you need to run somewhere.

Sound familiar? Sure. It is what most people are afraid is going to happen when they get in front of a crowd. Many, if not most, people think that this is somehow an unnatural phenomenon that only happens to them. But do you now see how perfectly natural it is? All of these symptoms are a direct result of what is happening chemically inside the body. Prior to any kind of performance we call it "nervousness" or "stage fright." Later we will take a look at methods to control these physical reactions and harness the energy they produce.

Research suggests that social fears and behaviors are also ancient inherited mechanisms, much like our stress-response system. They seem to be a part of our human physiology.[2] The theory is that our systems were wired for a time when the hierarchy of our social structure was determined by sheer physical dominance. Therefore, a person would be either totally subservient to the most dominant individual in the group, or be ready to challenge that ruler, and, in so doing, perhaps face injury, banishment or death. Considering the hostile nature of the world eons ago, the act of banishment itself could, in all likelihood, result in death. So it is not much of a stretch to imagine why, even to this day, so many people fear drawing attention to themselves, especially attention from superiors.

Additional evolutionary logic suggests that human babies quite naturally have a built-in fear of strangers and staring. This fear helps protect them from would-be abduction or harm by other humans or wild creatures. Being weak and defenseless, the infant's only chance of helping save itself is to cry like the dickens and hope that Mom or Dad gets there quick!

Fears about being judged, looking foolish, and possible rejection, all fall within a general negative state called "shyness." This is not a particularly scientific term, but certainly one many can relate to. In fact, it is reported that only seven percent of U.S. citizens say they have never experienced shyness![3]

Dr. Philip Zimbardo, a social psychologist from Stanford University, has done a great deal of work in the field of shyness.[4] He says that most people will naturally approach new activities with a low profile and will hesitate to do anything to call attention to themselves. This serves as another natural form of protection and allows a person to check things out to see if they are safe before diving right in and possibly getting hurt.

Parents and Family

Our parents, quite naturally, have a huge influence on how each of us develops socially. Some psychologists suggest that parents who have an extra measure of shyness will, in fact, pass this predisposition on to their children genetically. However, it is difficult to isolate that potential genetic factor from the social effects of the way in which a child is raised. If your parents, for instance, did little entertaining of guests within the home or did not relate well to other people, you would have had few opportunities at a young age to observe social interaction among adults. On the other hand, the kid whose parents entertained a great deal would have a much better background in adult social customs and banter.

Similarly, the size and closeness of one's family seems to have an effect on how shy a person will become. If, from birth, you are surrounded by brothers, sisters, grandparents, aunts, uncles, and cousins, you will witness and participate in countless social interactions on your way to adulthood. Eating, talking, laughing, telling stories, playing games, watching sports, dancing, singing and other activities done within the context of a large family, all help prepare a child for relating successfully to the rest of the world. Contrast this with an only child or a child with elderly or inactive parents, or latchkey children who may spend more time alone each day than with other kids. Socialization for these children depends a great deal more on activities outside the home.

Cultural Differences

Cultural norms play a part in how socially aggressive or shy someone will be. In Japan, as a case in point, the threat of bringing shame upon one's self and family has been historically used as a means of getting people to do what they "should." Transgressions, poor performance, or failure is considered a disgrace. According to Dr. Zimbardo, Japan has the highest incidence of shyness among all the countries he studied. Israel, conversely, has the least amount of shyness. This difference is attributed to the marked contrast between who is blamed for failures and who is credited for successes.

The Japanese, by in large, feel that *individuals* are responsible for their own errors. Achievements, however, are attributed to one's family, teachers, or the Buddha. However, a different view is taken in Israel. Accomplishments are more apt to be credited to individual initiative, while failures are blamed on external factors such as inadequate training or unfair competition. The Israeli child winds up having little to lose and much to gain by trying something new or different. The Japanese child, on the other hand, has little to gain and much to lose, so will therefore hang back, not be as aggressive about trying new things, and will generally take fewer risks.

Other East Asian countries have harsh social philosophies to control the behavior of individuals. For example, in Cambodia there is an adage, which when translated means, "The nail which sticks up will get hammered down." In that culture it is not wise to be noticed or rise above the rest. It is better to keep one's head down and be part of the masses. Individual effort, expression and achievements have historically not been encouraged.

A friend of mine, whose father was of Korean ancestry and mother of Japanese descent, says that when she was a child growing up in Hawaii her father did most of the talking around the house. She and her siblings were expected to keep their voices down and speak very little. It was this same way in the home of her Chinese friend. When the two of them were enrolled in a mostly Caucasian private school, they were amazed at how much everyone talked. "It was *so* noisy," she recalls. The white children, who were used to speaking with their parents on a regular basis, had a much easier time adjusting to school and the expectation of teachers that all students would participate in class and converse freely, answering and asking questions as needed.

Parenting styles and cultural norms in most Western cultures fall on a spectrum somewhere between the Israeli and Oriental philosophies. It is easy to see then, why we can turn out so differently from each other.

Peers

As children, our social development and self-esteem are influenced greatly by people our own age. Pressure to conform is a constant worry for kids. We want to be the same as everyone else and not do anything "dorky" to draw negative attention our way. Only the strongest and most confident youth can rise above the competitive snipping and sniping that goes on in the halls and classrooms of our schools. Generally, if children do not fit the mold their age or social group thinks is acceptable, they are made fun of until they conform. If they can not or will not conform, they are often banished from the group and labeled a "dweeb," or some other hurtful expression. (Sadly, this often happens among adults as well.) For someone who is already on the shy side, such treatment can be a devastating blow to their self-esteem and can adversely affect them for the rest of their lives.

Labeling

Children are of course very impressionable. They will accept much of what they hear from others as fact. When a young person is told by a classmate that he or she is a "geek," at some level this will be believed. Child-to-child verbal abuse of this nature is unfortunately extremely common; so too is negative labeling of children by adults.

Unthinking, uncaring or stressed out adults can inflict heavy damage on the ego of a child with words like: "Don't be stupid!" "That's idiotic!" "Quit being a crybaby!" "Shut up and sit down!" We have all heard such utterances and many beleaguered parents and teachers are ashamed to admit that these phrases have, on occasion, passed their own lips during times of overload. After cooling down, embarrassed and caring adults will apologize and try to make things right with the young person they have verbally abused.

Unfortunately, it is common for adult conversations to unwittingly, and without malice, label children who are within earshot. Every day millions of conversations take place between adults about young children who are nearby. Have you ever heard a discussion similar to the following example?

"Hi Bob! Lisa, take your thumb out of your mouth and say hello to Mr. Johnson. Stop hiding behind me! I'm sorry Bob. She's just *so shy*. I don't know why she acts like this. She's fine around the house, but when she gets out among strangers she goes into a shell. I don't know what's going to happen when she starts school. Kids can be so mean. They'll eat her alive!"

There are many adults walking around carrying labels that were placed on them during childhood and adolescence. Labels are extremely sticky and once used, they are very hard to remove.

We obviously cannot change our genetic encoding, cultural heritage, the selection of our parents, the size of our family, or the way in which we were raised. Whatever is in the past is gone. Yesterday is over. It is history. But the events of all our yesterdays shaped us into who we are today, spiritually, intellectually and emotionally. In that shaping process called *life*, some of us just happened to get an extra dose of shyness or stage fright.

While we cannot change the past, we can certainly change how we view and react to the world today. Each of us can make changes in who we are and how we feel about ourselves. Interestingly enough, no one else can. We are each in charge of our own destiny, if we will only allow ourselves to believe it.

Once you begin believing that only *you* are in charge of your future, then you can make significant strides toward personal goals such as being a confident and effective communicator. Through it all though, some of your natural fear will remain and you will have to work to control it. But as you will see in the pages ahead, fear is *not* an altogether bad thing.

*"Courage is resistance to fear, mastery of fear
–not absence of fear."*

— Samuel Clemens

— *Chapter 3* —

Study famous people who overcame insecurities

◆◆

*"Inherently, each one of us
has the substance within to achieve
whatever our goals and dreams define.
What is missing from each of us
is the training, education, knowledge and insight to
utilize what we already have."*

— Mark Twain

It may comfort you to know that many people who make their living being the center of attention used to suffer from insecurity and stage fright before they discovered the exhilaration of what would become their life's work.

The fact is, most people who make their living performing *still* get nervous even though they have faced countless audiences and cameras. But they make it look so easy, don't they? Sure. It is their job. But in order to appear natural and relaxed, and deliver seemingly effortless performances, professionals have to study and practice.

In a television interview several years ago the host mentioned to actor **Burt Reynolds** that he seemed to have a free, relaxed style in virtually everything he did. Reynolds thanked him and said he was glad that all of his hard work had paid off. He went on to explain that his movie and television persona was by no means natural. In fact, he used to be very shy and nervous, so he had to put in extra effort to achieve success.

While at Florida State University Reynolds was an outstanding football player and was being scouted by professional teams like the Baltimore Colts and Detroit Lions.[5] But an injury changed all that. He would never play football competitively again. This devastated him for a time because playing football was his dream, his passion.

With football behind him and looking for some new direction in his life, he enrolled at a junior college. Most of the classes he wanted were already full, so he signed up for art appreciation and English literature. Arriving late the first day of class, he found himself sitting in the middle of the front row under the watchful eye of the professor, whom Reynolds would later describe as his best teacher ever.

The professor, who was also head of the drama department, saw potential in the young ex-jock when the class read Shakespeare aloud. He decided Reynolds would become an actor and instructed him to show up for a play tryout, even though his new student wanted none of it. However, Burt was never one to duck a challenge. Despite the fact that he had no confidence in himself, he showed up and read the part. He spoke so softly he could barely be heard, but he got the part anyway. Once on stage Reynolds said, "Something clicked." After that he enjoyed the challenge of participating and wanted to prove himself.

It wasn't long before his talents were recognized and his television and movie career took off.

Henry Fonda, as a boy was a very unlikely prospect for the stage or screen.[6] Bashful and self-conscious, he often went out of his way just to avoid having to say hello to a girl. When he got to high school he was still sheepish and blushed easily.

But like Burt Reynolds, Fonda was coaxed onto the stage. At twenty years old he tried out for a part at the Omaha Community Playhouse, talked into it by the mother of another future super star, Marlon Brando, who was just a baby at the time. After a shaky beginning Fonda continued reading his script. Finally the director stopped him and told him he had the part.

Fonda was too shy at the time to tell anyone he did not know how to act and did not want to act. So he just mumbled to himself as he took the book and headed for home, where he memorized the part.

His first play only lasted one week, but that was enough to hook him on acting. At the opening performance of his next play a feeling swept over him, which he said made his skin tingle and the hairs of his neck stand up. It was the first time he realized what acting was all about. And it occurred to him that for someone who doubts himself this was a terrific thing to do. When you are an actor, other people tell you what words to say, what to wear and where to stand. So you are able to step outside of yourself and become someone else for a while.

In his delightful book on public speaking[7], newsman **Charles Osgood** relates how in 1972 he suffered through his first ever appearance anchoring a network news program. Even though he had been doing local radio for years, he had just recently moved over to the CBS network.

One Saturday he got tapped to anchor the televised CBS Evening News. Suddenly he found himself having makeup applied to his face and sitting under hot studio lights in Walter Cronkite's chair! That first time in front of the cameras, Osgood says he was "uneasy, self-conscious, and *bad*."

Another famous newsman, **Mike Wallace**, happened to catch Osgood's debut and offered some sage advice: "Don't act as if you'd wandered in off the street and were violating somebody else's property. *You* are in charge. Act that way." To this Charles Osgood adds the point that you need to "make it *your* lectern, *your* room." Osgood also advises us to always be ourselves and be real. Engage an audience individually and as a group, speaking directly to them, not just reciting words. Identify with them and enjoy what you are doing, because if you don't, they won't. In regard to stage fright Osgood says that newsman **Edward R. Murrow** called it "the sweat of perfection."

Someone who used to be in the news regularly, **Lady Bird Johnson** (brought into the public eye by her husband's political prominence as President) suggested that in order to overcome shyness you should "become so wrapped up in something else that you forget to be afraid."

Alec Guiness, Anthony Hopkins, Carol Burnett, Barbara Streisand, and, let's face it, just about every performer who has ever opened up and talked about themselves, admits to periods of fear, self-doubt and extreme challenge.

One actor had speaking difficulties as a child. He actually stopped speaking for eight long years. But he went on to become a marvelous stage and screen actor and the most popular and recognized voice in the entire film industry. His name— **James Earl Jones.**[8]

James did not have an idyllic childhood. His father left the family; his mother sank into drugs and alcohol, and he ended up being cared for by his grandmother. They lived in Mississippi, but about the time he was starting school the family moved north to Michigan.

Coming from the Deep South he did not talk like the other children. In the first grade, classmates started making fun of him. He began to stutter, then withdraw, and soon stopped speaking altogether. For several years, up to the age of fourteen, he was essentially mute. He became a loner, introverted and unhappy, observing rather than participating. He only occasionally said anything to his family, preferring instead to talk to their farm animals or himself. If a stranger came to the house he became petrified, unable to even introduce himself. Reflecting on those early years he said he had a strong desire to speak but simply could not.

When entering high school James was still mute. There he met a man, a retired professor, who became his teacher of English, Latin, and history. The teacher encouraged him and together they discovered something. Even though his severe stuttering made it almost impossible for James to talk in front of others, he could recite the written word fluently. Using this knowledge, the old professor and young Jones worked together to help him regain his power of speech.

James began devouring Shakespeare and Poe. His self-confidence grew, and he began to like himself once again. After all those years of silence he was able to burst into the open with a newly found passion. He could not get enough of being on stage in front of people and using his voice in acting, debating and speaking. He soon became a champion high school public speaker. His love for the spoken word never faded.

James Earl Jones went on to become a professional actor on stage, in television, and in the movies. The many awards he has received include Tonys, Emmys, Golden Globes, a Grammy and an Academy Award nomination. Jones, with his deep, melodic voice always speaking perfect English, is truly an inspiration to anyone needing to overcome a problem associated with public speaking or performing.

So the next time you see a *Star Wars* movie and hear his resonant voice portraying bad guy Darth Vader, or see him in *Field of Dreams*, *The Hunt for Red October*, or his many other works too numerous to list, realize *this* is what is possible. If you want something badly enough and work hard enough, you can have it.

"Attitudes are more important than facts."
— Dr. Karl Menninger

— Chapter 4 —

Free yourself from a negative "inner voice"

◆◆

*"Practice confidence and faith
and your fears and insecurities
will soon have no power over you."*

— Dr. Norman Vincent Peale

Having a positive self-image will take you a long way toward being comfortable speaking in front of people. To develop and maintain a good self-image requires that we deal with the negative inner voice that can plague each of us at times. It is important to know that even though what other people say to us, or about us, can impact our lives positively or negatively, nothing anyone else says can have as much influence over us as we have over ourselves. Why? Because we are with our own thoughts and opinions twenty-four hours a day every day of our lives. That is a long time—especially if you do not feel good about yourself, and if that little voice inside your head is always dishing out negativity.

Let's do a comparison. Consider for a moment how much you learned between entering the first grade and graduating from high school. Do you remember the teachers and coaches you had? There are, no doubt, at least a few who profoundly impacted your life. But you were not with any one of them for very long—probably one to three years at most. Doing the math, a child who is in class six hours per day for 160 days per year, will, over a twelve year period, be with teachers about 12,000 hours. Of course many of these teachers are positive, upbeat individuals who encourage and try to inspire students.

But, your internal voice has access to your psyche 24 hours each day, 365 days a year. So if you were to drag a poor self-esteem around for 30 years, this is like being home-schooled by a lousy teacher for over 260,000 hours—the equivalent of 270 school years!

It is difficult to move ahead with one's life and take on new challenges if you are constantly hearing phrases inside your head like; "You can't do that. You're too afraid. Why try? Don't even bother. You are not good enough!"

Good grief! Does any of that junk sound familiar? If so, it is time to make some changes.

How do you feel when you are around negative, whiny people who always see things in the worst possible light? It gets depressing, doesn't it? And if you are continually around a Grumpy Gus or Negative Nancy with a "poor-me" attitude, some of that is going to rub off on you every day. You may even become one of these people. Perhaps you already are!

But it is never too late to change.

To start the process, coldhearted as it may sound, you need to spend less time with negative people. You cannot make positive changes if what you hear all day long, both internally and externally, are negative comments.

Next assess who in this world can be of help to you and benefit your desire to improve yourself. Spend more time with these people. Surround yourself with positive people and positive ideas, and soon, instead of seeing barriers in your way at every turn, you will see infinite possibilities.

Seek out and experience joyful people and activities at every opportunity. This does not mean you should go quit your job or school, reject your entire past, become a full-time hedonist, and move to a tropical isle in the South Pacific. (Although on dark rainy days this might not seem like a bad idea.) Instead, slowly but unalterably commence filling up your life with *positives*. Start doing things that feel good and are good for you. Take a walk in the park, smell the flowers, pet a dog, and listen to the birds. Start a new hobby, or take up an old one that you once loved. Meet new people, and develop friendships with those who are upbeat, confident, and interested in your well-being. **If you concentrate every day on being positive, you will be able to create something out of thin air that perhaps never existed before: a clear vision as to who you want to be and what is really important to you.**

Once you begin establishing or reestablishing this vision, you will find that you are more focused, self-satisfied and proud.

When you reach this point, your inner voice will change. The loud negatives that used to lash you constantly will tone down and taper off to a mere whisper. Replacing the old worn out mockery will be words like, "Hey, I'm not so bad after all. As a matter of fact, I'm pretty good. I have valuable ideas. What I have to say is important and could benefit others. I should speak up more often." When you begin hearing *this* kind of talk in your head, you will know you are moving in the right direction.

There are many books available which can help you come to terms with a pesky inner voice and help you begin focusing on positive outcomes. One of these is a little book entitled *Timeless Wisdom - A Life-Changing Quotation Book*[9] compiled by Gary W. Fenchuk. It is filled with wise sayings about subjects such as living life to the fullest, realizing one's potential, positive thinking and taking risks.

Another book, filled with truly timeless wisdom, has been around since 1952 and sold well over 15 million copies. It is *The Power of Positive Thinking*[10] by Dr. Norman Vincent Peale. If you open your mind and heart to what Dr. Peale has to say, you will gain immeasurable benefits from his book and will feel changed by his words, which will help you develop the confidence necessary to communicate more openly with fellow humans in the world around you. As Dr. Peale says, "How we think we feel has a definite affect on how we actually feel physically."

Concentrate on succeeding - instead of *not* failing. Often, try as we might to be positive, we wind up shooting ourselves in the foot by focusing on mental images of things we do not want to have happen.

EXERCISE

Let's do an experiment. At this time do not think about a watermelon lying in a parking lot. Okay, now that you are not thinking about this watermelon, do not think about an elephant walking across the parking lot. Now that you are not thinking about either a watermelon or an elephant, do not think about what would happen if the elephant stepped on the watermelon.

So what did you just visualize? Red pulp, juice and seeds squirting out from under the pachyderm's foot—right? Do you see what happens? If you concentrate on what *not* to do, you wind up putting onto your mental radar screen the *very* images that you were trying to avoid. Focusing on what you don't want to have happen will clutter up your mind and get in the way of what you *do* want to accomplish.

EXERCISE

Let's do another visualization. You are now a speaker due to walk on stage in about five minutes. You are trying to mentally prepare yourself to do a good job. Consider what it would be like if the following paragraph described your feelings and thought patterns at that moment.

"I don't want to be too nervous. I don't want to forget what I'm going to say. I don't want to get distracted and trip on those stairs going up to the podium, and I don't want to drop my notes, and make a fool of myself. I don't want a tickle to form in my throat. I don't want the audience to fall asleep and Lord I don't want them to boo or get up and walk out in the middle of the talk because I'm such an idiot and they hate me!"

Whew! Nice image, eh? It makes you want to run right out and give a speech doesn't it? Or at least run right out. Richard Carlson, Ph.D., lecturer, consultant on stress and happiness, and author of the book *Don't Sweat the Small Stuff...and it's all small stuff* [11], refers to this type of thinking as the "Snowball Effect." The longer it goes, the larger and more menacing it becomes and the harder it is to stop. Another highly technical term sometimes used to describe this type of thought pattern is "stinking thinking."

Now let us consider a quite different way of thinking before you face a crowd.

"My preparation, breathing and physical exercises have helped me relax, yet I have plenty of energy to do a good job today. This seems like a nice group of people. I should be able to connect with them quite well and give them some excellent information they can use. My thoughts are going to flow freely, and my voice is going to be clear and strong. This will be a good presentation today. They will probably invite me back.

I'm glad I am here!"

What do you think? For most people the second paragraph feels much better.

Perhaps you are a person who has trouble visualizing success, but somehow picturing failure has never been a problem for you. Because of this you may have held yourself back from things you were not sure you could do, like public speaking. If this is the case, you might be able to learn a lesson from *Very Worried Walrus*.[12]

In this popular children's book, Mr. Walrus could not bring himself to even *try* riding a bicycle because he got so worked up over what *might* happen if he fell off. He visualized all kinds of calamities. He saw himself falling off and getting injured. Then he was picked up by an ambulance, which crashes on the way to the hospital. Then a helicopter picks him up and *it* crashes into a river. But a boat picks him up, and, of course, it sinks, putting him in even worse peril. Dr. Carlson has another term for this type of mental torture we sometimes put ourselves through. He calls it a "thought attack."

Not until Mr. Walrus quieted his "thought attack" and summoned the courage to actually get on the bike and try it, did he realize that riding is fun! And then, when he did inevitably fall off, he found out it wasn't that bad. So he just got back on and tried it again.

So don't be a "Worried Walrus." When you develop a mind-set that good things are going to happen, there is an excellent chance they will. Think positive thoughts and visualize absolute success every time before going in front of an audience. If it turns out your complete vision does not come true, so what? You gave it your best shot; you survived; you learned from the experience; and you will do better next time.

"I'm happy to be here! I'm going to do great!"

A winning attitude like this really works! It is a wonderful gift you can give yourself. So be a winner, and start focusing today on *positive* outcomes. Focus on what you want, not on what you used to be afraid of. Focus on succeeding, instead of not failing.

Be tough with your inner voice.

As you begin tackling fears and progressing, be mindful of what your inner voice is telling you. If it is being positive and encouraging then keep doing what you have been doing. But if you hear negativity creeping back with phrases like "I can't," then get tough with yourself. That negative voice will hold you back, so you cannot afford to let it hang around.

If you do suffer a setback and start getting down on yourself, stop and ask why. Think about what it is that is bothering you and consider what it would be like if you were to stop your progress and go back to the way things were. Consider why you have hit this rough spot and, whatever the reason, break the cycle of negativity as soon as you can. Take five. Change what you are doing. Breathe in some fresh air and reaffirm to yourself that you are going to be okay and that only *you* are in charge of your own destiny.

John Milton declared, "The mind is its own place, and in itself can make heaven of hell, or hell of heaven."

To experience real change and successfully meet new challenges, that negative little voice must be drowned out by a positive one. To this you may declare, "Okay, I'll try." But, as Dale Carnegie said, "Don't try. Do! There is a difference between trying and doing. If you only commit to *trying* you have not committed to much" ...and your fear is still in the driver's seat.

"Don't try. Do!"

- Dale Carnegie

— Chapter 5 —

Play the role of a confident person, and you will become one

◆◆

"All the world's a stage, and all the men and women merely players."

— William Shakespeare

We play numerous roles in the course of a lifetime. In fact, we routinely play several roles all in the same day—child, parent, employee, boss, friend, neighbor, and many more.

One role many of us take on at an early age is that of someone who fears being the center of attention and fears speaking in front of others. We often reinforce this role by telling ourselves and others, things like; "I'm afraid to speak in public. I just can't do it. I get too nervous." This role, or way of seeing ourselves, can have long-lasting impacts on our lives. It can affect how we view the world, with whom we form relationships, what we do for a living, and how we spend our free time. In short, playing a fearful role can in many ways direct how a person's life evolves.

Quite naturally, people who are fearful of being the center of attention will often choose fewer social activities to engage in and may also choose career paths which require fewer communication or leadership skills.

But what if you changed your attitude and decided you want to play a different role? Is that possible? Yes, it is. You just have to give yourself permission.

But how do you feel about your ability to take on a different role? It is possible you have played the same role for so long that you have stereotyped yourself, and now believe that you cannot change. It happens—just like Hollywood actors get typecast as good guys or bad guys, and then find it difficult to break out of those roles. The same is true for the rest of us. However, our fate is not in the hands of movie moguls. We control ourselves, so *we* get to decide what roles we will play.

You might not believe it at this moment, but there is no question that you *can* change. You can take on a different role—the role of someone who can speak confidently in front of others. You may have feared public speaking for a long time, but you *can* do it.

Imagine your reaction if someone told you today that two days from now you would stand up in front of 100 people and make an impassioned, convincing speech that would move all of them to action. Your reaction might be to say "No way! I couldn't do it. I wouldn't do it. No one could *make* me do that!"

Okay. You may indeed make such declarations today, but you would be wrong. Because given the proper set of circumstances you would, without consideration for your past fears, step up and give an effective, impassioned speech and get people to act. I will prove it to you.

EXERCISE

Picture the following: you are on vacation in a beautiful port city and decide to take a ferryboat ride. As it happens there are four classrooms of grade school children on board taking a field trip and you are on the same deck with them. The children are taking snapshots of each other, and everyone is enjoying the nautical sights and sounds—whitecaps on the water, boat whistles, and the cries of seagulls as they circle overhead.

Suddenly the ferry hits an underwater obstruction! The vessel is jarred as a large gash is ripped in the bow below the waterline. The ferry begins taking on water rapidly. Astonishingly, on impact all of the teachers and aides responsible for the entire group of school children were knocked unconscious. None of the ship's crewmen have made it to your location yet. So at this moment, you are the only adult left standing on deck, surrounded by a mass of frightened, screaming children. To save their lives you need to act immediately by standing up on a bench and saying in a loud, authoritative voice:

"Everyone be quiet!! Listen to me! You are going to be all right. I want you to calm down; form a line; and grab a life jacket from this cabinet. Then go stand by that railing and wait for instructions. You big kids help the smaller ones and then come help me with the teachers. Okay? Let's do it **now**!"

If all you had to do to save the children and their teachers was give this 20-second long, 60-word speech, would you do it? Of course you would! Without hesitation you would assume the roles of speaker and leader. You would give that impassioned speech to 100 people and convince them to follow your directions. All this, despite the fact that a minute ago you doubted you could give such a speech. Would you be nervous? Possibly - but most likely your concern for the children would be your focus, and you would ignore any nervousness as you set about doing what had to be done.

The truth is, we are all capable of doing much more than we think we can. We can take on new roles that we have never played before if we put our minds to it. No one was born a network news anchor, entertainer, or riveting public speaker. The skills and abilities necessary to pursue these or any other dreams must be learned and practiced. But in order to improve ourselves and grow we must constantly go outside of our personal comfort zone. To move from where we are to where we want to be, we need to stretch and feel a little uncomfortable, a little nervous—sometimes a *lot* nervous. We need to challenge ourselves mentally and emotionally just as we do physically when it comes to exercising and conditioning our bodies.

For some, taking on the role of being a confident public speaker is going to be more difficult than for others. Some initially will find it challenging to even say their name in front of just two or three people without becoming embarrassingly red-faced. For others their threshold of uncomfortableness will be higher, say five or ten people. Still others may not be challenged until asked to present a three to five minute speech to fifteen or twenty people. For those at a more advanced level, it may take an even larger audience or longer speech to really give their nerves a workout.

If you are ready to move on though, ready to change, ready to become more confident in front of a crowd—there is little value in hanging back and doing only what comes easy. You must stretch yourself by getting out and trying new things.

Projecting Confidence

What is it that sets a self-assured, confident person apart from others? What habits have they developed that are different? Can we pick a person like this out of a crowd? Often times we can, merely from external clues. What kind of an image do *you* currently project? Do you display as much confidence as you would like? Many of us could use a booster shot in this regard.

Let's look at a few of the clues that tip us off to the fact that a person is confident and self-assured. As you read through these, imagine what it would be like if you exhibited these same characteristics every time you were in public.

Good Posture

A self-assured person will walk with head held high and shoulders back, displaying pride in who they are, instead of hanging their head and slouching.

High Energy

Confident people have a spring in their step, move along a little more briskly than others and exude energy and purpose, instead of slowly shuffling along mumbling to themselves.

Eye Contact

Eyes are generally up and scanning ahead. There is more interest in where one is going than where one has been. Occasional eye contact is made with others. If you never look people in the eye it is as though you don't care about them. They might as well be a lamppost or fire hydrant. If that is how other people think you feel about them, what kind of energy will they feed back to you? Probably about as much as a lamppost or fire hydrant would. Eyes are the windows to the soul. If you do not allow anyone to peer into them, no one will ever know the real person behind them.

Voice

Speech is clear and understandable. Mumbles, grunts and groans are not the hallmarks of positive, upbeat people.

Physical Appearance

Good grooming habits and a fashionably appropriate manner of dress says to the world, "I care about me." Confident people tend to like themselves, so they want to take care of their personal assets. If a person does not care about him or herself, it is unlikely anyone else will.

Positive Attitude

The self-assured will project a feeling that they are doing exactly what they want to be doing. They are more apt to be smiling and greeting those around them and may occasionally be heard whistling while they work. Instead of slinking off to hide from the world, these people try to grab each moment and make the most of it. And they know that they cannot always control what happens to them, but they *can* control how they feel about it.

Back in school your teacher decided when you were ready to move on to new challenges. But now, *you* must decide. Are you up to trying a new role? If so, it is now time for you to play the role of a confident, self-assured person. Of course, you may not feel that way yet, but *act* like it anyway. (This is not to suggest that you become arrogant and self-centered. These are traits of people who feel that the only way to lift themselves up is by putting others down.)

Start small

Pick out a role model or two and begin doing what they do. Act like they act. Incrementally, day by day, take on the traits of a confident person. Dress well. Use good posture. Display high energy and enthusiasm in whatever you do. Connect with people using your eyes and voice. And *always* find the positive elements of any situation you find yourself in.

As you begin adopting these characteristics you will begin to feel differently about yourself and you will find that others will begin reacting differently to you. By changing your outward appearance and demeanor you will modify the world's perception of you.

In case you haven't noticed, people are drawn to those who are positive and confident, like bugs to a porch light. So as you act more upbeat and confident you will find yourself making more friends and acquaintances. The more new people you meet, the more comfortable you will become meeting even more people. It is a wonderful, positive, upward spiral. Before long, the *role* you started playing will become *reality*. Soon you will not be "acting" self-confident anymore. You will *be* self-confident!

"Our self-image and our habits tend to go together.
Change one and you will
automatically change the other."

— Dr. Maxwell Maltz

— *Chapter 6* —

Calm yourself through proper breathing

◆◆

"Instead of frittering away
your vibrancy with worry or distraction,
realize your mind and body are inextricably united.
What calms and tones up one,
soothes and improves the other."

— Marsha Sinetar

After struggling unsuccessfully with a problem for a long time, it is not uncommon to feel defeated and want to give up. But if we take complex problems and break them down into manageable parts, they are less overwhelming. Stage fright is such a dilemma. Looking at the whole, it just seems too difficult to overcome, and each year that we put off dealing with it makes the problem seem all the more menacing.

But there are little things you can begin doing right away that will help you be more at ease in front of people and better able to speak publicly when the need arises. Learning to breathe properly is one such example.

Deep breathing is a terrific relaxation technique that can be used whether standing in a crowded room or sitting at a table with a group of people. Have you ever noticed how taking a deep breath can sometimes make you yawn? When you start feeling nervous, or even before then, straighten your back and breathe in through your nose, filling your lungs completely. Hold this breath for a few seconds, then slowly exhale through your mouth. Do this several times, taking in nice big breaths. Expand your diaphragm fully. If you are breathing properly your belly is going to be extended slightly with each inhalation.

For many people, when they take in a deep breath, their chest will rise while their stomach stays flat. For vocal performances though, of which speaking is one, this is not the correct way to breathe. To help you understand why, let's look at human anatomy for a moment.

The diaphragm is a large thin muscle, which curves upward. It fits snugly against the bottom of the lungs and separates the chest cavity from the abdomen. For you to take a breath your diaphragm must contract, which makes it move downward. This creates a slight vacuum in your chest cavity that causes air to pour into your lungs.   During inhalation your diaphragm flattens out, instead of being curved upward. As your diaphragm flattens it pushes down and out on your digestive organs.

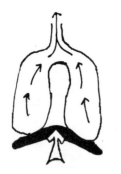 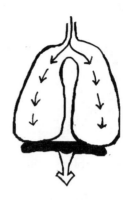

Relaxing diaphragm pushes air up and out

Diaphragm contracts to pull air down into lungs

However, if you have acquired the habit of holding your stomach muscles tight, then the natural process of breathing is stifled. Instead of your abdomen being extended slightly, your chest will rise. When you are speaking or performing, this kind of "chest breathing" is undesirable—for two reasons. First, it results in shallow breaths, which may cause you to run short of air in the middle of a long sentence. Secondly, people can see more easily when you take a large breath, which may give away the fact that you are extra nervous at the start of a presentation. The following demonstration shows you why this is true.

EXERCISE

Stand in front of full-length mirror or one in which you can at least see your upper body. Concentrate on your face, as an audience would. While looking in the mirror, stand up straight and relax your stomach muscles. Also relax your arms. Let them hang naturally at your sides. Now take in a large amount of air, and let it push your abdomen outward. When you release the breath your abdomen will go back in. Do this a few times. Notice that while concentrating on your face this deep breathing is barely noticeable, because your chest and shoulders remain stationary.

Next hold both hands firmly over your abdomen and tighten your stomach muscles. Now take in a huge breath of air and observe what happens. Not only does your chest rise, but so do your shoulders and arms. Taking a deep breath in this manner is not only inefficient, because you won't completely fill your lungs, but it also makes it obvious to an observer that you are taking a large breath.

To check yourself occasionally for proper breathing technique, borrow a trick from singing coaches. Place a flat hand lightly over your navel, and take a deep breath. If your belly swells with each inhalation, you are breathing correctly. By learning to breathe correctly, not only will you be calmer, but also you will have plenty of air for speaking, singing, acting or any other type of vocal performance.

As your diaphragm pulls down to inflate the lungs, your abdomen should be allowed to expand outwardly to make room for adequate air.

— Chapter 7 —

Work through fear, and it will no longer control you

◆◆

"They conquer who believe they can.
Do the thing you fear and the
death of fear is certain."

— Ralph Waldo Emerson

As much as it makes us feel uncomfortable, and we wish it would go away, fear is a mechanism that actually *protects* us from harm. If we had no fear we would be much more apt to fall out of windows, get bitten by dogs, and run over by buses. So fear is not a bad thing. The downside of fear is that it limits what we are willing to try. Therefore, even though it is a personal safeguard, fear will often hold us back beyond reason, keeping us from enjoying life to its fullest and accomplishing all that we are capable of.

Dr. Susan Jeffers, a psychologist and popular public speaker, has written a book in which she tells her own story of conquering fear. In her book, Dr. Jeffers gives excellent advice centered around a theme, which is also the book title, *Feel The Fear And Do It Anyway*. [13] Dr. Jeffers is quick to point out that her book has nothing to do with taking foolhardy chances and risking one's life or the lives of others. Jumping off the Golden Gate Bridge or driving on the wrong side of a freeway, for example, would not be things to fear but do anyway.

What Dr. Jeffers does in her book is to dispel the notion that there is something wrong with us psychologically just because we have fears relative to normal events in our lives. Many of us are fearful of asserting ourselves, or introducing ourselves to strangers, or standing up to make a public presentation. But if we continue to simply avoid activities like these out of fear, our lives will be much poorer because of it. Imagine all of the opportunities that could pass you by if you weren't willing to grab onto them. To avoid limiting yourself and being held back by dread, work to reduce your fears little by little until they are at a manageable level.

But how can I start doing something that I am afraid of?

The answer to this question is *gradual desensitization*. Put another way—"baby steps."

If a person is afraid of something, be it public speaking or anything else, it does not do them much good for another person to simply declare, "Oh, it's okay. Just stop being scared."

Let's say for example that you are deathly afraid of horses, but you want to overcome this fear and learn how to ride. It would be of no benefit for an expert rider to say to you, "It's nothing. Just hop up on that big gelding, nudge him in the sides and head down the trail." If you are extremely fearful of horses this is *not* something you are going to do. You may not even be able to get anywhere *near* that horse.

A better approach to gradually overcome your fear would be something like this. First, simply go and watch from a distance while horses are being handled. You could see how they are groomed, how they respond to people, what some of their habits and mannerisms are, and you could gradually get used to the sights, sounds and smells of being around horses. Eventually you would be able to move closer without feeling the intense fear you once had. Soon you could pet a horse's nose or his side. In due time you would be feeding the horse carrots and grain out of your hand. Before long you would be able to stand next to the horse and brush him.

Next you might accompany someone while they lead a horse around in a corral. When comfortable with the idea that the horse is not a danger to you, you could then take a turn at leading him around. After your basic fear was gone you could learn to properly mount a horse and sit in the saddle. A trainer could then lead the horse around in a corral while you rode. Eventually you could be riding on your own, first in a corral and then out on the trail, your fear of horses defeated.

By taking small, graduated steps we can overcome our fears, or at least reduce them to a level that we are no longer paralyzed by them. Anxiety about public speaking is such a fear that can be reduced and eventually overcome—one step at a time.

Get a little closer to your "horse" each day.

In Chapter 9 we will discuss very specific ways you can practice sneaking up on your fear of public speaking. For the moment though, consider this: in order to improve, from whatever level you are at currently, you are going to have to push yourself.

Day by day, week by week progressively put more pressure on yourself to experience ever greater challenges. Taken gradually enough, you will be able to feel your fear, recognize it for what it is, take a deep breath, and then proceed anyway. After having done that, reward yourself somehow. It doesn't have to be anything big—maybe just some time alone walking in the park reflecting on your success. But if you have bravely faced and met a significant new personal challenge, what the heck—treat yourself to a new CD, a trip to the movies, a nice dinner, or something else that will reinforce the importance of the accomplishment you just achieved.

When through celebrating, start planning for the next challenge you hope to take on. Each one will get easier and easier. Every time you successfully face your fear, reward yourself again. Through repetition and conditioned response you can train yourself to overcome the fear of public speaking just as surely as the family pooch can be taught to sit for a dog biscuit. Crazy as it sounds, you can eventually come to love the very thing you now fear.

Fear and self-doubt are not an easy duo to deal with—especially when we are so used to living with them. But once you begin to quiet this pesky pair you are going to be able to seize new opportunities, to speak up, and get more of what you want out of life. Your dreams will begin to take shape, and you will begin to experience clearer thought patterns. Your mind will not be constantly racing worrying about what someone else thinks or feels about you. The thoughts and feelings of other people are theirs and theirs alone, and all the worrying in the world is not going to change anyone or anything. So try not to worry so much about what other people think. Save your energy for more productive endeavors.

French novelist Albert Camus once said,
"What doesn't kill me makes me stronger."

— Chapter 8 —

Use nervous energy to your advantage

◆◆

"If a man acts fearless long enough he will eventually become so by repetitive practice."

— Theodore Roosevelt

Nervousness is a seemingly negative trait. But it is not. In fact, we can turn nervousness into something very positive and make our natural fears work *for* us instead of against us. There is a common misconception that before anyone can become a good speaker or performer they need to totally rid themselves of nervousness. So most of us go through life believing that as long as we continue to feel tense and have butterflies before getting up in front of people, we cannot possibly be successful with an audience.

As it happens, this belief is entirely incorrect! Actually, a certain level of nervousness is not only desirable, but is absolutely essential. The good news is that nervousness is not fatal. It simply heightens your awareness and gets you ready to perform. So don't resist your nervousness. Flow with it. Understand that there will be times when you feel uneasy, but know that once you get started the uneasiness will subside. What will remain is the energy you need to do an excellent job for your audience. How can you do the best job for an audience? By being alive and showing excitement. A vibrant, energized, enthusiastic speaker is almost impossible to ignore. Nervous energy is needed to fuel this kind of performance. So embrace your energy. Move to it. Feel the tension and excitement. Next time it will be easier. Eventually, if you do it often enough, you can develop a liking for the adrenalin rush and euphoria one gets from doing anything exciting or daring, like running a race or driving fast.

All of us, even professional speakers and performers, experience symptoms of nervousness. The difference is, professionals recognize the reactions taking place in their bodies as normal processes and, through practice, have learned to turn these to their advantage. Dr. Norman Vincent Peale, a premier twentieth century speaker, once said, "I always get nervous before I stand up in front of an audience because I have a profound respect for people. The responsibility makes me a bit nervous." What a revelation! The suggestion that nervousness comes from feelings of respect and responsibility is foreign to most of us. But it is true. If we care about others, then we want to do a good job for them. We do not want to let people down or waste their time. We want to give them our very best.

So before giving a presentation of any kind, it is only natural for us to worry about whether we have prepared enough and whether we are going to do a good a job. These thoughts will manifest themselves in feelings of intense nervousness. This same nervousness will provide the fire in your belly that is needed to adequately prepare and present a stirring, animated performance which will grab and hold an audience's attention. It does not matter if you are addressing grade school children or upper level corporate executives. Lively, fervent presentations result when nervous energy is used to pump out positive thoughts, words, emotions, and actions.

To help illustrate why it is essential to maintain some level of nervousness, let us consider what it would be like if a speaker experienced absolutely *no* tension at all before or during a presentation. There have probably been times in your life when you have run into such totally relaxed people, even though they may be addressing a crowded room. Have you ever attended a lecture presented by someone who you suspect has given the same talk for ten or twenty years without updating it? They undoubtedly had the material down cold, and could probably have given the presentation in their sleep. But were they enthusiastic? Full of life? Inspiring to listen to? Did they hold your attention? Probably not, on all counts. Chances are you had to conceal droopy eyelids behind a cupped hand while pretending to take copious notes.

Sometimes speakers are *too* at ease and they lose their edge —an edge that comes from respecting an audience and wanting to give them something really worthwhile. So savor the edge that you have when you are nervous, wondering if you have all the latest facts, if your props are ready to go, and if your audiovisuals are going to do the job.

As a speaker, if you do not have enough energy, your audience will drift away mentally, and sometimes *physically*. Empty chairs after a break is a sign that adjustments are in order. So hallelujah for nervous energy! Without it your speech could be a flop because your audience could be asleep.

If asked to make a presentation, don't duck out of it. And if you are nervous about it—good! That means you *care* and you are stretching and progressing toward your goal.

Overrelaxed versus nervous... yet expressive.

**"People don't mind if you're nervous.
They do mind if you don't care..."**

— Frank Sinatra to fellow crooner Tony Bennett,
when Bennett was a young performer.

— Chapter 9 —

Seek opportunities to practice

◆◆

"Skills to do come of doing."
— Ralph Waldo Emerson

An out of breath man running down a New York sidewalk suddenly stops and asks an elderly gentleman, "Quick, how do I get to Carnegie Hall?" The old man sagely responds, "Son, you've got to practice, practice, practice." The same is true for learning how to speak publicly. Like anything worth doing, if we want to be good at it, we must do it often. But first, we must simply get started.

Using our horse metaphor once again, let's say you want to learn to ride. At some point you are going to have to get in the saddle, take hold of the reins, and invest time practicing. This is of course true for anything we want to become skilled at. No one can learn to drive a car by simply reading the owner's manual. So when it comes to learning how to reduce anxiety and be an effective speaker—guess what? You are eventually going to have to practice.

But where? There are all kinds of opportunities available. You may not have noticed them before because you weren't ready to. There is an old Chinese proverb that says, "When the student is ready the teacher will appear." Now that *you* are ready—ready to start learning and practicing the art of public speaking—possibilities are going to begin springing up all around you.

Let's explore some examples of what those possibilities might be. First we'll look at a few baby steps you can begin taking. Then we will proceed toward more advanced levels, which will require you to progressively summon more courage. Keep in mind, the more often you experience fear, but proceed anyway, the faster you will get your anxiety under control.

First Steps

Attend meetings. If you fear even *being* in a group setting, then just walking in the door of a large meeting hall filled with people might be *your* first step. Your second step might be to attend another meeting, and then another. Attend lots of meetings and community gatherings where you can get used to the feel of various crowds. While you are there, take note of how emcees, chairmen or presenters behave while they are speaking or otherwise in charge of the meetings. Perhaps most importantly, begin visualizing yourself as a successful speaker at one of these gatherings.

Attend parties, or throw one. Relaxed social settings provide opportunities to tell jokes and stories to small groups of friends, acquaintances, and sometimes complete strangers. Whether we recognize it or not, this is a form of public speaking. Observe people who have a knack for smoothly working a room, breaking into and out of conversations and telling funny anecdotes. You can learn from them by watching their body language and gestures, and listening to what they say and how they say it. When you feel comfortable, dive in and join the conversation. If you begin telling a funny story and start getting some laughs, before long an audience of ten or twelve may gather to listen to your humorous presentation.

Answer or ask a question. Some day soon—perhaps at work, school or elsewhere—you will be in a meeting or some other kind of interactive group situation. Your baby step in this case may be to speak up and answer a question posed to the group or say something like "I didn't understand that last point. Could you go over it one more time please." That's just fifteen words. Words which probably half of the room will thank you for saying, because if *you* are confused, others are undoubtedly confused as well.

Bigger Steps
Take a class. If you are attending school, sign up for a speech class. If you are not in school, there are still opportunities available for you to learn public speaking through community education classes, seminars and various series such as Dale Carnegie, Fred Pryor, and others.

Join *Toastmasters International*. For anyone who is serious about overcoming stage fright and improving his or her public speaking skills *Toastmasters International* is <u>highly</u> recommended. *Toastmasters* is a nonprofit, self-help organization with over 8900 clubs worldwide made up of people from all walks of life. They come together for an hour or so each week with a common purpose—to become better communicators.

The men and women of *Toastmasters* learn and practice public speaking and leadership skills in a friendly, supportive, setting. An experienced speaker/mentor is typically paired with a beginner to encourage and help guide initial progress. One of the real beauties of the *Toastmasters* organization is that everyone works at their own pace. Dues are minimal—only about $25.00 for six months. That is less than a dollar per week! Included in that price is an easily understandable training manual and a very informative monthly magazine.

By working through the manual, speakers can literally advance from novice to expert. To find a club near to where you live check your local phone directory or the Community Calendar Section of your newspaper or call the *Toastmasters* national office at 1-800-9WE-SPEAK, send an email to: clubs@toastmasters.org, find them on the Web at www.toastmasters.org, or write to them at Toastmasters International P.O. Box 9052, Mission Viejo, California 92690-9052.

Sign up with *any* kind of club. Service Club, Booster Club, Hiking Club, Garden Club, you name it. They all have officer and committee positions that need filling. Here is a low-key way of getting consistent speaking experience, meeting new people, perhaps making a contribution to your community, and having fun.

Volunteer. In virtually every community, urban or rural, there are opportunities to volunteer. Public and private nonprofit agencies are always looking for help. Some examples would include museums, zoos, the Forest Service, Park Service and Fish and Wildlife Service. Approach any one of them and explain that you would like to volunteer so you can acquire speaking experience. You might be surprised at the offers you will receive.

Giant Steps

Try Community Theater. Okay, *this* opportunity to get up in front of an audience may be about the farthest thing from your mind right now. But do you remember the experiences of Burt Reynolds and Henry Fonda? They didn't think they would like it either. For those who want to progress rapidly at getting comfortable in front of an audience, theater is a great place to do it. Here you will find training, opportunity, and supportive new friends. Plus, you get to practice speaking in front of people as someone other than yourself, using a playwright's words instead of your own. Community theaters are filled with fun-loving, hard working volunteers who enjoy sharing their craft with others. Frequently there are very small roles, both speaking and nonspeaking, that a person can try just to see if they like it. If you are interested, check your local phone book and give the theater manager a call.

Learn to say "Yes" to public speaking opportunities. As you become more comfortable in front of people, one way to rapidly improve your speaking skills is to accept as many offers to make presentations as you possibly can. Once the word is out in your company or community that you are willing to get up in front of people and talk, you *will* receive invitations to speak—because almost everyone else is as fearful of public speaking as you *used* to be!

Push yourself to speak regularly, even if just a little bit each week. By taking advantage of speaking opportunities at your place of work, in school, at various meetings, dinner parties or wherever, you will build a solid foundation of success from which to continue your growth. To become a competent public speaker put pressure on yourself to expand your horizons and go outside of your comfort zone. As you become more proficient look for new challenges and opportunities to consistently sharpen and maintain your skills. Before you know it you will have such a background of speaking experiences that you will almost forget why you used to get so nervous in front of people. Hard to believe? Maybe. But true!

"What we hope to ever do with ease,
we must learn first to do with diligence."
— Samuel Johnson

WARNING!!
Some people won't want you to change.

As you begin to work through your fears and begin to change and project more confidence, people are going to notice. As they do, you will slowly begin to find out who supports you and who does not. Supportive friends, family and coworkers will encourage positive changes in your life. But be forewarned, there may be those, perhaps someone very close to you such as a spouse or other relative, a friend, or maybe your boss, who will fear the changes they see in you. For their own reasons, some people may discourage your progress.

Why? One reason may be that people get used to filling certain roles and having those around them in other roles. So when an individual starts to change, that upsets the status quo. For many of us, change is uncomfortable. Those who are the most bothered by your new-found success may try, perhaps without even being aware of it, to reestablish the old order of things and derail your positive changes. If this happens, you must summon the courage to simply advise them that you are moving forward with your life and have no desire to go back to the way things were.

Standing up for yourself and honestly telling people exactly what you think, how you feel, and what you need, can be difficult—extremely so. But it is important to learn how to do it. If you need assistance in this area Dr. Jeffers' book *Feel The Fear and Do It Anyway* is a good reference.

Learn to lean on your network of family, friends or coworkers who support the positive changes you are making for yourself. For additional help perhaps you will want to talk things over with a clergyman, counselor, or personal coach. Also look to libraries, the Internet and bookstores. There is much that has been written and is available to you on the subject of fear and how to cope with it. Go out and find the resources that work best for you and start making the changes you know are necessary. Do not let others dissuade you from advancing just as far as your intelligence and fortitude will take you.

Part Two

TO BE AN
EFFECTIVE SPEAKER...

— Chapter 10 —

Get yourself ready

◆◆

*"Seventy-five percent of victory depends
on preparation."*

— Dr. C.E. Matthews

Have you ever committed to doing a presentation, then written it, rehearsed it, and been on the way to deliver it, when panic set in, and you said to yourself, "Yikes!—What am I doing?" That's okay. This is a common reaction. A good example of this was when a nationally known outdoor writer friend of mine was once on his way to give a speech in Alaska. He was flying at about 30,000 feet when suddenly dread swept over him. He secretly wished for the plane to crash—figuring his chances with a rough mountainous landing, grizzly bears and wolves would be better than having to face an audience. But the plane landed safely, and so did his speech. After it was over he looked back, laughed and wondered what all the fuss was about. Your presentations can have a smooth landing too if you adequately prepare.

Know your material

Go over your material numerous times so that you know it well and know about how long the presentation will take. Rarely should you read a scripted speech, unless precise wording is necessary. Most of the time you will to want to use a minimum of notes and present information in your own words. But using fewer notes will require that you put in more practice time.

There are three items in any speech which are appropriate for memorization. These are the *opening*, *key points* and *closing*. While it is seldom critical to have these down word for word, it is good to at least have a strong grasp of where you are going with them.

For example, imagine what it would be like if a speaker said, "So ladies and gentlemen, I would like to emphasize that **the** most important issue at hand is…" (At this point the speaker pauses to look down at notes.) Do you see what that brief pause did? No matter how stirring the speech may have been up until that moment, the speaker gave away some credibility by not having the closing statement down pat. The closing *should* be the real punch line of any speech. And we all know what it is like to forget the ending of a joke. "No wait. Let's see. How did that go again?"

Now while it is appropriate to memorize some parts of your speech, it is generally advised that you never try to memorize the whole thing unless it is a classroom assignment or you are acting in a theatrical production. Occasionally you will see a speaker start out articulately, impressing their audience with big words and complex sentence structure, despite not having any notes. Then suddenly they stop, perhaps with a bit of panic on their face. Why? Because they are trying to remember the next word or line. At this point it may become apparent to all that the speaker memorized the entire speech verbatim and was thrown off the script for some reason. This can happen sometimes by missing a single word or being distracted by a little thing like a sneeze or a slamming door. Herein lies the greatest reason for you to *not* precisely memorize an entire speech. You may get lost in the middle of it.

When you practice your speech you may want to do it out loud in front of a mirror. This will help you "see" the speech somewhat as your audience will, complete with body movements and gestures. Or, depending upon your circumstances, you may only be able to go over the presentation in your mind and mentally visualize what gestures and movements you will use. Whichever method you choose, if at all possible, prepare and rehearse in a quiet area where you will not be disturbed.

See Part III for details on speech preparation.

Settle down

To avoid getting all worked up and nervous about making a presentation, commit the following three facts to memory and go over them in your mind each time before you give a speech. It will help you be more at ease.

1. Nervousness is normal.

Not only is nervousness normal but, as you read earlier, it is essential for a good performance. So don't be afraid of being nervous. Turn it into an advantage and use it to help produce a lively, memorable speech.

2. We *feel* more nervous than we *look*.

No one can see your butterflies. *You* know they are there

because you can feel them, but it is like winking in the dark. No one else knows you are doing it unless you tell them. So never feel obligated to apologize to an audience for feeling nervous. Just energetically dive in, and work through the first few moments of your speech. As you do, things will begin to smooth out, and you will settle into a comfortable groove.

3. People *want* you to succeed.

Audiences want to witness success. They don't want to see anyone squirm and be miserable. It may be them up there someday. So whenever you need to stand before a group of people and make a presentation, realize that everyone is silently pulling for you. Audience members will often remark, "I wish I was brave enough to do that." So take comfort in the fact that most listeners appreciate your efforts and envy your courage.

Physically prepare

To prepare your body for a performance and be as physically at ease as you can, do two things—*warm up* and *burn off excess energy*.

1. Warm up

To avoid strain or other injury, a baseball pitcher will warm up his throwing arm before a game. As a speaker, you need to warm up muscles and connective tissue which control the various elements of your voice.

Vocal cords are actually fibrous ligaments attached to muscles. If these are not warmed up properly, your voice may be scratchy and not perform at its peak. What is your voice like when you answer the phone in the middle of the night after being jolted awake? Sometimes it takes a moment or two to be understood, doesn't it?

If you do too much, too fast with your voice (like many fans, players and coaches at sporting events), then the voice may be temporarily strained. Do this often enough and permanent damage may result. This is a problem which singers take great care to avoid.

So take the advice of voice coaches: exercise your "instrument" before a performance. You can do this on the way to your engagement simply by talking. If possible though, work the full range of your voice by doing musical scales at various volumes. The idea is to warm up gradually. This is particularly important if you will be addressing a large audience and will not have the aid of a microphone.

Probably few people outside the entertainment world ever think about warming up their *facial* muscles. As acting and voice coaches will tell you, it takes the whole face to make the sounds of speech. The warmer and more relaxed these muscles are, the better they can perform. Following are a few exercises that may sound and look funny while you are doing them, but they will loosen and warm up your facial muscles and make it easier to perform the tasks of projection and pronunciation.

The Lion's Roar Open your mouth as wide as you can for a few seconds and feel your face and neck muscles stretch. Then close. You don't have to make any noise with this, unless you want to scare your neighbor or the guy sitting in the car next to you at a traffic light. Repeat this a half dozen times or so.

Motorboat We all did this as kids, and you can still hear it today on kindergarten playgrounds everywhere. Purse your lips together loosely and force air out between them. This will give your lips a good warm up.

Rolling R's The tongue vibrates while you roll your R's making an rrrrrrrr sound. If you are doing it correctly you may sound a little like a Harley Davidson motorcycle. This is a hard exercise for some people to do. For others though it is second nature, as this is a basic sound of some languages. If the concept of rolling R's does not make sense to you yet, just ask for a demonstration from someone who speaks Spanish or Italian, or who sings classical music.

Tongue Twisters Reciting a few of these several times in sequence will help keep you from tripping over your tongue when you hit a word that is hard to pronounce. Some old favorites include:

Ma, may, me, moe, moo.

Rubber baby buggy bumpers.

Peter Piper picked a peck of pickled peppers. If Peter Piper picked a peck of pickled peppers, how many pickled peppers did Peter Piper pick?

How much wood could a woodchuck chuck if a woodchuck could chuck wood?

2. Burn off excess energy

As discussed previously, excess nervous energy is often what gives away the fact that we are experiencing stage fright. This energy can build up in us and result in shaky hands, a quavery voice and other familiar symptoms. There are ways to effectively combat this problem, which are well-known to professional speakers, actors and others in the public eye. The secret lies in *movement*.

Movement helps burn off excess energy. Let's think basketball for a moment. At the start of a big game adrenalin is pumping and all the players are keyed up. The first few bricks they throw up at the basket provide evidence to this fact. But within minutes everyone settles down. Passes get crisper and shots begin to consistently drop through the hoop. Why is this? It is because the players have burned off excess nervous energy and can now get in the flow of the game.

A similar thing happens to speakers. Before starting a talk, adrenalin begins flowing and tension builds. But unlike the athlete, who will soon be running, jumping and elbowing somebody, a public speaker generally cannot do those things, at least not in a dignified manner. So what can be done? The answer to this question is a major trick of the performing trade.

Famous stage and screen actor Yul Brenner played the leading male role in the Broadway production of *The King and I*. He did so for four thousand, six hundred and twenty five performances— 4625! Surely, after the first hundred or so times of doing a play, a professional actor is no longer going to get pre-performance jitters, right? Wrong! Like Dr. Norman Vincent Peale, Mr. Brenner respected his audiences and wanted to do the best possible job he could for them. So every night at showtime his adrenalin would start pumping. Like any actor he *needed* this adrenalin to give a sterling, animated performance that could bring down the house. However, similar to an athlete before a big game, he would have *too* much adrenalin in the beginning. Brenner's solution was push-ups, but not on the floor. **Waiting backstage for his entrance cue, he would lean into a wall and do more-or-less vertical push-ups.** Exercising this way, he burned off surplus energy and was better able to focus on details of his upcoming performance.

How else can we burn off excess energy? An old favorite of many is pacing. Any physical exercise will help—walking, jogging, jumping jacks, knee bends, and others. But what if it is not possible to do any of these things before a presentation? What if, for example, you are just one of a number of people sitting at a head table waiting your turn to speak? You may *want* to jump up and run around, but you can't. What then?

Not to worry; there is a sneaky solution you can employ, which even the person sitting right next to you will not notice. It is called *isometrics*, and it really works. By pushing muscle against muscle you can burn energy anytime, anyplace, in any position while remaining absolutely motionless.

Try this: in whatever position you are in right now, tense up your stomach muscles. Keep them tight, but keep breathing, just taking shallow breaths. Without releasing your stomach muscles, tighten up your thighs. Now hold these tight while you tighten up your chest and arm muscles. Still breathing (and with a smile on your face), hold everything tight for a ten count, then release.

Whew! That can be a workout, can't it? In tensing your muscles just then, you were perhaps burning more energy than if you had been pacing or doing wall push-ups.

Try these other techniques:
- While in a sitting position push your knees together.
- Cross your legs at the ankles and pull out on your legs.
- With your hands folded in your lap, push your palms together.

Depending on circumstances you can mix and match some of these for good effect. By flexing major muscle groups you can burn plenty of energy to help yourself relax—all the while sitting in public, seemingly composed and thoroughly at ease. The first time you pull this off, you are not only going to feel proud of yourself, but you'll feel a little sneaky too. "Ha! They didn't even know I was nervous!"

Check your appearance

Wear clothes that are appropriate for the occasion. If you are not sure what the manner of dress will be, ask someone. Keep in mind that as a speaker it is better to be slightly overdressed than under-dressed, but you don't want to be in a tuxedo or evening gown while everyone else is casual.

Unless you are familiar with a particular group, make few assumptions about how they are going to dress. If speaking to the local carpenters' union at an evening meeting, do not assume they will come straight from work and be in overalls and tool belts. They probably won't be. Unless they are at work, few people will wear their "uniforms" to a meeting. This goes for carpenters, baseball players, surgeons, and most of the rest of us.

It has been said, "Worry gives a small thing a big shadow." So do a final check in front of a mirror before walking out into the limelight. This will reduce your worry about what may or may not be undone or out of place. Check yourself from top to bottom every time, and you will be less apt to miss something. Plus, it never hurts to ask someone else, "How do I look?" They may say, "You look great, except for the long thread hanging off of your elbow and the spinach in your teeth."

In case you happen to miss something that is askew, like perhaps a critical fastener on your wardrobe, there is no need to panic. Just deal with it when you need to, and, if necessary, laugh along with the rest of the world. We are all just human. When we look at humor in Chapter 13 you will see how TV comedian Johnny Carson dealt with one such embarrassing situation.

Concentrate on your audiences' needs

As you prepare a speech, your ultimate goal should be to satisfy the needs and wants of your audience. When stepping to the front of a room, you may see a *crowd* in front of you, but what is important is how you connect with all of these people as *individuals*. They, not you, should be foremost in your mind. Their needs should take center stage. What do they need? What can you give them? How can you help them?

Once you have made this mental shift, then busy yourself capturing and holding the attention of audience members, so they will get the most out of your presentation. **You will find that when you focus strictly on the needs of others, there will be no time left to worry about yourself or your fears.**

And that is a good thing because it will begin to spell the end of that bedeviling nuisance we call stage fright.

"Worry gives a small thing a big shadow."

- Anon

— Chapter 11 —

Take control, use gestures, and show emotion

◆◆

"Always give them the old fire,
even when you feel like a squashed cake of ice."

— Ethel Merman

Eventually, everyone is given the opportunity to take center stage. When your time comes, seize it. This is what all the preparation leads to. When introduced, nervous or not, move quickly and confidently to the front and play the role of a self-assured speaker. By exuding confidence you will have what is called "stage-presence," which is an attitude really.

When approaching the window of a car that has just been pulled over, police officers exude a certain "presence." By doing so, they take command of the situation. Similarly, NBA basketball referees also must project confidence and authority when about to go nose-to-navel with angry seven-foot three inch, 325-pound basketball players.

Like the cop or the referee, you, as a public speaker, must take control and resist the urge to think, "This is too scary. I can't do it." Instead, assure yourself, "I will handle this situation and do it well." By projecting an assured demeanor, people will sense you have something important to say, and they will *listen*.

At the beginning of a speech, despite your best preparation, you may still experience more nervousness than is comfortable. If this happens, just remember, the audience does not have x-ray vision—except maybe for that guy in the back wearing the cape and blue tights with a big red S on his chest. But the rest of us mere mortals can not see your nerve endings. So the only way anyone will know that you have a case of the jitters is if you tell them or tip them off by doing things which make you look nervous.

In this chapter we will focus on how to take control of an audience, how to appear calmer than perhaps you really feel inside, and how to hang onto an audience's attention and effectively communicate with them.

Seize the stage

However you choose to do it, seize control of your audience right away. Your challenge is to get each audience member to stop thinking about the rest of his or her life for a while and concentrate on what *you* are saying. After all, you have something worth listening to. So approach it that way. When it is "showtime," move to the front as though you cannot wait to get up there. Immediately be loud enough with your voice and broad enough with your gestures, so the audience knows that you are now in charge. Leave no doubt in their minds. Don't even give them the opportunity to think you may just be someone wandering around looking for something or testing a microphone. Take control!

One group of speakers who really have to do this is lounge entertainers. Bars and nightclubs probably have the loudest, most distracted audiences anywhere. So what do most stand-up comics do when they first come on? They rapidly go downstage center, look straight at the audience and loudly say, "Hey! How's everybody doin' tonight?" This gets most everyone's attention and many people will answer the question. Still in motion, the comic may speak directly to another section of the crowd asking a second question. "You all havin' a good time?" Now he or she has everyone's attention. Of course, most of us are not going to open a presentation as though we are stand-up comics. But our challenge is the same however—to get people to stop what they are doing and pay attention to what we have to say.

Move around and don't try to hide

Many speakers would like nothing more than to get behind a lectern or podium and hide until their speech is over and all of the people have gone home. You know the feeling. We all do. Initially it may seem cozy and safe behind that big chunk of wood. But staying back there creates some problems that may not be readily apparent. For one thing, it presents a physical barrier between you and the audience. You may think, "That's good! They can't wing me with a tomato if I stay back here." However, barriers are precisely what you want to eliminate when trying to communicate with people. The more barriers you can remove, the more attentive people will be. And the more closely people listen, the more they will absorb of what you are saying.

Coming out from behind that fortress has other benefits as well. The simple act of moving burns energy. What is it we usually have too much of at the beginning of a presentation?

Nervous energy! So get rid of some of it. Walk around while you talk.

It may help you to know that by moving around you are also going to assist the audience to stay focused on you and your message, because movement is hard for the eyes to resist. Also, you will automatically appear more relaxed and inviting for the audience to listen to. Look at TV talk show hosts. When do they appear the most relaxed? It is when they are up and moving, either doing a monologue or walking amongst the audience chatting.

Now it could happen that a stationary microphone or other factor will someday force you to stay in one place, such as behind a lectern or table. But if this is the case, there is still much physical movement you can do in the form of gestures.

Gestures

How we say something often communicates as much as what we say. When talking face-to-face we constantly exchange nonverbal cues with each other in the form of facial expressions, how we position our body while sitting or standing, and how we move our upper body, including head, neck, shoulders, arms and hands.

The use of gestures is a means of communication unique to cultures and individuals. Regardless of one's typical gesturing style, there are times when speaking situations will be enhanced by exaggerating these movements. For example, when in a large room, lecture hall or auditorium, motions need to be more pronounced to match the space. The bigger the room, the broader your gestures should be. Remember, keep the audience foremost in your mind and use whatever gestures or movement is needed to focus listeners on what you are saying. If people are not focusing on you, they will be lost to other thoughts. ("I need to pick up a gallon of milk, a loaf of bread and one other thing. Hmmm, what was it?")

If listeners start getting a faraway look in their eyes, snap them back to the present! Grab and hold their attention by bringing variety to your gestures. Physically portray the emotions of your speech to put power in your presentation. If you are communicating anger, then clench your fists, grit your teeth and bang the lectern. If you want to display tremendous joy then put on a huge smile, throw back your head and spread your arms out wide. For despondency—frown, stick out your lower lip, pull your limbs inward, hunch your shoulders and walk slowly. To be childlike, skip around swinging your arms and your head back and forth. To be very old, stoop slightly and pretend you have a cane or grasp pieces of furniture to steady yourself as you shuffle by them.

To put maximum pizzazz into your gestures, become an observer of people and their many moods and movements. Then recreate these for your speech, making them as broad as needed, so even the person in the very back row can interpret what you are doing.

Posture

It is important to have good posture when you are speaking. This will maintain proper breathing and you will present yourself as professional and confident. Standing up straight with your shoulders back and chin up, combined with broad and rapid gestures, will give you a confident demeanor. On the other hand, if you slouch, keep your head down, shuffle your feet, and use only small, slow gestures, people may get the impression that you are shy, nervous, or standoffish.

When giving a presentation you of course want to appear relaxed, but you also want to look and be alert and attentive. If you are using a lectern, chair, stool, table or other piece of furniture, resist the temptation to lean on it. Some speakers will tend to drape themselves over a podium, but leaning heavily on something might be interpreted by your audience as tiredness or boredom with your own message. People may be tempted to doze off or finish their grocery list.

Eye contact

An absolutely essential tool for a speaker is good eye contact with audience members. Constantly sweep the room with your eyes stopping often, but momentarily, to make direct eye contact with individuals. Once an audience realizes that you are interested in talking to each and every one of them individually, they will listen to you as individuals. This is an important concept. Your job is not to talk to the back wall, the ceiling, your shoes, the flip chart, or just a sea of faces out there. Your job is to communicate with individuals.

Whether there are two or two thousand, never think of your audience as a mob. Instead, see them as distinct souls, hearing and mentally processing the information you give them, independent of one another. The visual connection you make with each person, however brief, will reassure listeners that you care about them personally. Constant eye contact will also reassure you, as the speaker, that the audience is a group of normal humans, just like you, who care about what you are saying.

Use Emotion

The more emotion a speaker brings to a presentation, the more a listener will take from it. If offering up only bland facts and figures, a speaker can expect to get little response. But weave that same information into an emotional, interesting story, and you will serve up a memorable speech. And what people remember, they can <u>act</u> upon.

The challenge to each of us is to overcome our reluctance to display emotions publicly. This is a fearful thing for many people and probably one of the biggest hurdles our psyches have to jump over on our road to improved public speaking.

We have all had experiences, some good and some bad, which will elicit strong emotional responses if we dwell upon them—the birth of a child, the loss of a loved one, an honor bestowed upon us, a wartime experience, or childhood trauma. Whether joyous or painful, most of us know which memories are closest to our emotional core. We also know about how far we can go in talking about these life-changing events before our emotions start to rise to the surface. It is at that point we generally break off a conversation and change the subject, for fear that we may display our emotions.

But what if we want to have maximum positive impact on other people's lives? What if we want to help others deal with

Engage your audience and keep them involved:

Ask questions

Make questions to the audience real, not rhetorical. This reminds everyone that you are not just talking to yourself. If you ask a real question and no one answers, ask it again. Let the audience know that you know they are out there and that you can tell when they are listening.

For example, if addressing a group at a workshop on speech anxiety you might say, "I used to be nervous for weeks in advance of giving a speech. Does anyone here have that problem?" Chances are you will see many nodding heads and get various forms of yes responses. You could then ask follow-up questions like, "Would anyone like to share with the group why they are here today?" At this point if everyone clams up and looks at the floor, you might (for their own good) have to single out a few of the braver looking souls to get things going. "How about you? Could you tell me your name?" Then follow with questions like: "Where do you come from? How long have you lived there?" Those kinds of questions are fairly innocuous and will get a person loosened up and talking about him or herself. Then you might slip in; "Can you tell me one thing you hope to get out of today's session?"

Call for a show of hands

This can be silly or serious. "How many people got stuck on the bridge in reconstruction traffic this morning?" Even if you have just flown in from the opposite side of the country, by recognizing and mentioning a local situation, an audience will instantly connect with you. Asking for this kind of show of hands is a good way to start making that connection.

The best way to get people to participate in hand raising is to come right out and ask them to. With your hand high in the air you might say, "I'd like to see a show of hands from all of you who have ever experienced stage fright? Okay, for those of you who have had stage fright (which is most of us) how many of you ever worried that you were somehow abnormal because of your nervousness about getting up in front of others?"

Engaging people in this manner, with a show of hands, will not only get audience members relating to you as a speaker, but they will also start relating better to each other and develop a higher level of trust.

Get them on their feet

Maybe you are following one or two other speakers and it is not yet break time, but the audience's posteriors tell them it is. You will be the hero of the hour if you take it upon yourself to get everyone out of their chairs for a one minute stretch break. An added benefit is you have just subtly conveyed to everyone that you now have control of the meeting. Be prepared, however, to assert yourself strongly at the end of the break to get the room quieted down and everyone back in their seats. You might say, "Okay everyone, please take your seats. I have some important information to share with you." If you have planned ahead you might add, "And I've got treats for the quick learners!" Then start tossing a few small candies to audience members who are already seated. (Careful though—I accidently lobbed one into a guy's cup of coffee once which splashed up on him. He was a good sport about it though and didn't even sue me.)

Another ingenious thing you can do is a combination of getting people on their feet and responding to questions. To overcome the fear many people have of bringing attention to themselves by raising a hand or standing up, turn the tables on your audience and ask everyone to stand up. Once the whole group is standing, then start your series of questions and ask audience members to respond to them by sitting down. For example you might say, "All those who never experience stage fright, please sit down." Do you see how this can work? Asked in this manner, probably the whole room will remain standing, admitting openly to themselves, you, and the rest of the room that yes, there are times they are fearful.

But, if people were asked to stand in response to the converse question "How many of you experience stage fright?"— Perhaps half or less of the room would respond. Why? Because it takes more bravery and openness to stand up and be counted, than to simply remain standing with a group in response to a question. This is an excellent technique to use when you suspect people are going to be embarrassed and not give true answers if they are asked to stand or raise their hand in response to questions.

Ask for volunteers

Maybe you just need someone to turn out the lights or perhaps a helper or two on stage to aid with a demonstration. If no one volunteers, do it the old reliable way, "Could I please have you, you and you up here for just a moment." It is effective and keeps everyone else *really* awake for the rest of your presentation.

Have them "Repeat after me"

This too can be serious or silly. Use your imagination. At a session on fighting anxiety you might say, "Repeat after me: The next time"... (*audience echoes: The next time*), "I feel the fear"... (*I feel the fear*), "I will do it anyway." (*I will do it anyway.*)

Take a vote

A vote can be fun and instructive at the same time, and it can breathe new life into a presentation, particularly after lunch or in the late afternoon. In a workshop you might use this technique to get audience feedback and help steer the program so that attendees get the most of what they want.

In a speech workshop, for example, the instructor might say, "We have only an hour left, and there is much more I'd like to tell you. So I am going to give you some options; I will describe them to you, and then we'll vote.

#1 We can continue our discussion on causes of anxiety and stage fright.

#2 We can move on to a discussion of advanced public speaking techniques, including interviews and working with microphones and television cameras.

#3 We can have a long question and answer session and talk about anything that's on your mind.

So let's vote by applause. How many vote for #1?"

By getting people involved and having them help decide things, they will stay focused on the subject at hand.

"Don't ever let me catch you singing like that again, without enthusiasm.
You're nothing if you aren't excited
by what you are doing."

— Frank Sinatra (to his son)

— *Chapter 12* —

Maximize the quality of your voice

♦♦

*"You may be disappointed if you fail,
but you are doomed if you don't try."*

— Beverly Sills

Your eyes are the windows to your soul, but your voice is the doorway through which the world will come to know you. Voices are unique. Like fingerprints, no two are exactly alike. The voice is our most interesting and expressive means of sharing ourselves with the world. Imagine what it would be like to be mute, unable to speak, unable to spontaneously share your ideas with people. The thought of not having a voice gives one a bit more appreciation for how much we depend upon oral communication.

This chapter will first describe how we make the sounds that become known as our particular "voice." Then we will explore how the voice can be controlled and varied to more effectively communicate with an audience.

Anatomy

There are two ligaments in the throat, which are made up mostly of elastic fibers. These are called the vocal cords. As air from the lungs rushes up between these two cords, they vibrate to create sound. When stretched tightly they produce a higher pitch than when they are loose, much like a stringed instrument. Loudness of the voice depends upon the force with which air rushes across the cords, similar to a woodwind instrument. Perhaps the best analogy can be found as close as your backyard or nearest city park. If you pick a blade of grass and hold it lengthwise between your thumbs, side by side, and blow through the hole, air rushing past the grass will create a squeal. The tighter you stretch the grass the higher the pitch will be, and the harder you blow the louder the noise is.

Although vocal cords have the primary job of sound production, much of the quality and uniqueness of a voice is determined by the size and relative arrangement of other physical structures. Oral, nasal and sinus cavities give the voice a distinct tonal quality, while the throat acts as a resonating chamber and amplifier. Sounds are then shaped and given clarity and proper enunciation by the tongue, teeth, palate, and lips.

Volume

As speakers, we need to be constantly aware of whether or not we can be heard. Electronic amplification is not always available to give our voices a boost. So in large spaces we have to *project* our voices, so that the farthest person away from us can hear and understand what is being said. *Not* doing this is one of the most common mistakes speakers make.

This problem is compounded for people with small voices. Our challenge is to not be afraid to boom out when the need arises. The ability to do this will come with increased self-confidence and practice. Theater directors are often known to say, "Splat it off the back wall!" Of course you don't always have to be loud. Occasionally, bring your volume down to a lower level, so the audience has to pay closer attention to what you are saying. If you have a microphone, you can even lower your voice to a whisper for good effect.

Articulation

This is another aspect of speaking that has particular importance when in large, open spaces. The clarity with which words are pronounced will make the difference between simply being heard and being understood. Make your words crisp by clearly articulating your consonants. Slowing down will also help. If you are having trouble with this, practice with a friend or coach or tape yourself and become your own coach.

Rate

Generally, when giving a public address, your rate of speaking should be throttled back a bit from normal conversational pace. Many of us get carried away and start talking comparatively fast when we are among friends and family. But those who know us personally are used to our speech patterns. So we can get away with talking rapidly around them. Talking too fast while giving a presentation though will result in people whispering, "Did you catch that? What did he say?" While quizzing each other they may not hear the next thing you say. Soon there may be side conversations going on all over the room, and you won't know why. If in doubt about whether you can be heard and understood, ask the audience. They will tell you.

Pitch

Your voice may be as high as Bernadette Peters or as low as James Earl Jones. Pitch is fairly dependent upon personal physical features. A piccolo will never be as low as a tuba, and a tuba will never be as high as a piccolo. But there are exercises you can do to expand your vocal range. Singers use these exercises all the time. They would not be able to maintain their exceptional ranges if it were not for giving their voices frequent workouts.

So perhaps you have a very high voice and would like to broaden your range to develop a slightly deeper, more authoritative speaking voice. This can be done through vocal exercise. The very best way to get off on the right track and be sure to not injure yourself, is to work with a voice coach. This person can give you advice, precautions, and a few exercises to work on, then turn you loose on your own.

But if working with a coach is not possible for you right now, you may want to try exercising your voice by doing musical scales. Start in the middle of your range and work up and down the scale. Don't push it for the first week or two though. Only go for a few minutes and be sure not to strain your voice. Little by little with each daily session, after your voice is warmed up nicely, you can begin reaching for notes on each end of your range. Take it easy though—don't be in a hurry. You spent a lifetime developing the voice you now have. To modify it even a little is going to take time. If you have access to a tape recorder, read aloud occasionally and record yourself. In this way you can capture your "normal" voice for comparison purposes, and begin experimenting with the new voice you would like to have.

Vocal Variety

To make interesting presentations and stay connected with an audience, vary the rate, pitch, volume, and emphasis that you place on certain words or phrases. Strive for peaks and valleys, fast spots and slow spots. If the terrain of your voice is too flat, you will sound tired and monotonous. This is a trap into which many speakers fall, taking their audiences with them.

Another good way to spice up your speech is have fun with your voice. If you feel up to it, throw in a different voice once in a while. This can be done while you are telling a story or describing a person or event. You can make yourself sound like a little kid, an older person, a cartoon critter or other character voice. By totally switching to another voice for a moment, you jar the audience a bit. This perks them up, usually gets a laugh, and keeps them tuned in to what you are saying.

The more theatrical you can be with your voice, the more inclined people will be to keep their eyes and ears focused on you. As you give a presentation, pay attention to how closely your audience is listening to you. If you start to lose them, add a dash more vocal variety to reel them back in. Perhaps emphasize a point by saying it **LOUDLY!** Or start to talk very fast and then s l o w   d o w n. With experience and confidence you can have fun experimenting with your voice to grab and hold the attention of an audience.

Voice Placement

This is generally not something we think about when we are simply talking. However, "placement" is essential in musical voice training and voice-over acting for radio, television, and cartoon production. Placement deals with where and how sound is created and the resulting quality of the voice. Here are three examples of different placements. (These are much easier to demonstrate in person than they are to describe.)

Chest Open up your mouth and nasal passages and use a lot of air to support a big sound. This is a chest voice. A baritone opera singer would most often use a chest voice.

Throat Air from the lungs is restricted and not allowed to go through the vocal cords with full force. Sound is somewhat held in the throat. If you exaggerate this you can mimic the Munchkins from *The Wizard of Oz.* "We're off to see the Wizard..."

Nasal Either internally or externally (by pinching your nose) block the flow of air coming out your nose while you speak. By modifying the route that air and sound takes in getting out, the noise you emit is changed. This makes it sound as though you are stuffed up with a head cold.

There are numerous other voice placements that could be described. Suffice it to say though, by modifying the way in which you hold and release air and sound, and by combining various placements, you can vastly change the character of your voice.

Accents and Dialects

Obviously people develop speech patterns unique to their culture and geographic region. Our manner of speech serves us best when we are among family, friends and people who know us. But if we venture away from our neighborhoods a few thousand miles, or sometimes just a few blocks, we find that not everyone speaks the same language as we do. Pronunciations can vary greatly depending on where you are. When business or personal travel takes you away from home, you will eventually hear words pronounced in a way that have no meaning to you. Likewise, you will say things that other people, supposedly speaking the same language, will *not* be able to understand. For example, consider the different forms of English spoken in Los Angeles, San Antonio, Atlanta, Brooklyn, Kennebunkport, Winnipeg, Liverpool, Johannesburg or Melbourne.

Just be aware that we all have distinctive regional characteristics in our voices and in our choice of words and phrases. Because of this, other people will sometimes have difficulty understanding what we say. We can minimize this problem though, if we continually practice the use of good English and limit the use of hometown colloquialisms. Of course this may be hard to do, if you are *always* in your hometown. But it is worth the effort. To cite once again a great example, James Earl Jones, it would be very difficult for anyone to guess he was from Mississippi and raised in Michigan. He has done an excellent job of training his voice.

One way to impress an audience and get on their good side immediately is to properly pronounce their local geographic names—especially ones that most outsiders normally mispronounce. Conversely, butcher a key word or two and you will be doing damage control for a while, trying to get the audience back on your side. My home state, Oregon, provides an illustration. Many people from outside the Pacific Northwest pronounce it "Or'-gone." But any dyed-in-the-wool Oregonian will tell you it is pronounced "Or'-ee-gun."

It takes a little up-front research to avoid such faux pas. This is one good reason to arrive early before a speaking engagement. While checking out the lay of the land, tune in to the local lingo. This will help avoid a situation someday of stepping to a microphone and saying something like: "I wish to thank you for inviting me to your lovely state of *Or-gone*."

Voice Problems?

Many people do not like the sound of their own voice and because of this they are embarrassed to speak in public. If this describes you, seek out a second opinion from friends or colleagues. Listening to your own voice either from inside your head or on a recording device is of course not the same as listening to others speak. So ask someone, whose opinion you respect and who will take the issue seriously, what he or she thinks of your voice. Have an honest discussion about it. Your voice is uniquely yours and it is probably just fine. But if, after having examined it, you still feel there is an element of your voice that needs improvement then dive in and work on it. Perhaps you have a stutter or maybe your voice has a nasal quality to it. Many of these and other conditions are very fixable through speech therapy or voice training with a good coach. Don't stand in the way of your own progress. If you think you need to change some aspect of your voice, and especially if you are using that as an excuse to not advance your public speaking skills, get after it and start on some changes.

But keep this in mind too – some people are successful at using speech *imperfections* to create a personal distinctive voice. Will Rogers' homespun speaking style is a good example. He was not always grammatically correct, and he projected a very country persona when he spoke. But he was successful and people loved him, because he was "the common man." Studying the speaking habits of a variety of people may give you ideas on how to maximize the use of your own special voice.

Your voice is the doorway through which the world will come to know you.

— Chapter 13 —

Have humor

◆◆

*"I don't know jokes.
I just watch the government and report the facts."*

— Will Rogers

With humor you can break the ice, capture and hold people's attention, relax an audience, and put a dash of humanity into what otherwise might be a dull, factual presentation. Also laughter can keep an audience fresh and alert while they are still sitting down because the act of laughing causes people to work certain muscles, move around a little, and take in more oxygen.

Nothing will put you on the good side of an audience quicker than humor if it's appropriate for the occasion. Humor can immediately set everyone at ease, including the speaker. One good way to start is by poking fun at yourself with a bit of self-deprecating humor. Senator Edmund Muskie once began a speech by telling his audience he felt inadequate to stand before them with his humble presentation. He said, "I feel like a mosquito in the middle of a nudist colony. I don't know where to begin."

From My Own Experience...

I once witnessed a terrific motivational speech at a national convention in Albuquerque, New Mexico. The speaker, who was totally blind, received applause as he made his way to the stage escorted by his wife. She helped him get situated at the lectern and get his microphone on, after which she returned to her seat.

He started his presentation by thanking everyone for such a warm welcome. Then he said, "Let's see a show of hands: How many people here are from out of town?" About 90% of us raised our hands high. A huge grin came over his face, and the entire audience then knew the joke was on us. He couldn't see our hands! The meeting hall roared with laughter. With that, the speaker captured everyone's undivided attention for as long as he wanted to talk.

Unfortunately, many people never try using humor because they feel they would not be any good at it. "I can't remember jokes," some will say. But anyone can remember at least a couple of jokes if they are willing to put the time and effort into it. Jokes have to be practiced—just like other parts of a speech. And remember, we *are* allowed to use notes during speeches.

Others may lament, "I can't even think of any jokes to put in a speech." No big deal. That's what bookstores, libraries and the Internet are for—research. Even in relatively small libraries you can find dozens if not hundreds of categories of humor listed. And, needless to say, humor can be found within all categories of books, not just in the humor section. True stories found in biographies are some of the funniest.

"But I can't steal somebody else's joke," you might say. Well, tell that to the professional comics. They've been stealing each others jokes for years. Milton Berle used to make fun of his own proclivity to "borrow" other people's jokes. Look at it this way: by reusing a good joke we are paying tribute to the last person we heard it from. In fact, sometimes a funny story will get an even bigger response if attributed to a well-known comic like Bob Hope, Jerry Seinfeld or Rodney Dangerfield.

Tailor jokes to fit you and your audience.

Instead of just retelling a joke in its original form, tailor it to fit your particular situation. A hundred years ago great grandpappy may have told a real knee-slapper about a butcher, a baker and a candlestick maker riding in a buggy together. Regardless of the punchline, that same joke today could be about a butcher, a baker and computer chip maker riding in a Subaru.

Basic human nature and our sense of what is funny does not change all that much over time. William Shakespeare's comedies still get big yucks. You can find common elements of humor crossing from one generation to the next in material done by the likes of Jim Carrey, Tim Allen, Robin Williams, Lucille Ball, Milton Berle, Sid Caesar, Red Skelton, Abbott and Costello, W.C. Fields, Charlie Chaplin, Harold Lloyd and others too numerous to list. Sometimes it is hard to describe what makes us laugh, but we know it when we hear it, or see it.

"Bob Retires" – An Example.

Let's say you have been asked to emcee a retirement "roast" for your old friend and colleague, Bob. Okay, you need a few jokes. So head to the library and find some material you can tailor to the occasion and to Bob personally. In this way you will have some of the best joke writers in the world on your team. Make their jokes your jokes. Personalize them. Change names, dates and circumstances, so the stories come to life for your audience. Your presentation honoring Bob might start out something like this:

"Thanks for coming everybody. To get things started I thought I might just tell you a little about Bob's life. Bob was born at a very early age. Now as you all know, Bob has always complained that he didn't get any respect from any of us here at the office. Well that actually started the day he was born. When he first came into the world the doctor mistakenly picked him up by the wrists and slapped him in the face. Now I don't want to say Bob was an ugly child, but after the doctor got a closer look at him, he slapped Bob's mother. When Bob's father came in and got a look at his new child, he slapped himself!

Oh we kid Bob a lot, but we're glad he joined us here at the company 30 years ago. He's been a real asset to us. It's hard to believe that in his younger days a superior once accused him of being indecisive and lackadaisical. But Bob stood up for himself. He shot right back, "I'm not so sure about that, and furthermore, I don't care!"

But Bob has become a real decisive executive with the company. Decisions, decisions all day long. What to do, where to do it, who to blame. Bob really only had one problem here with the company. He hated reports. He used to say reports are like bikinis: What they reveal is interesting, but what they conceal is vital.

He read a corporate wellness report prepared about him one time that said cigar smoking, drinking and carousing were bad for a man's health. So he decided to do something about it right away. He gave up reading.

But seriously, we're sure sorry to see Bob go. But hey, look at it this way – we're not just losing a top executive, we're gaining a parking place and a desk to pilfer."[14]

You get the idea. Take jokes and fit them to your occasion. To do this effectively you need to know your audience, at least a little. You certainly do not want to use anything that is going to offend and put people off. Hard-hitting humor, like Don Rickles uses, can be risky. He often singles out individuals in an audience and talks to them or about them on issues like race, cultural heritage, clothing, weight and height. More often than not, Rickles gets big laughs with his jokes, but the rest of us might just get punched in the nose.

Creating your own humor.

As you get bolder and realize humor is not rocket science, you may want to put together some of your own material. There are humorous observations to be made everywhere you look. All you have to do is recognize something as funny and bring it to the attention of others. Talk show hosts and comedians make a living doing this.

If you want to strengthen your funny bone, make it a point to watch funny movies and tune in TV comedians. Observe the techniques you see and perhaps try to mimic some of them.

As a teenager, Groucho Marx honed his craft on vaudevillian stages with his wacky brothers and continued to do so in the movies. His rapier wit was so fast that a TV game show called *You Bet Your Life* was built around him in the 1950's. It ran for 12 years. To get a more modern sampling of his type of rapid fire observations and witticisms (all of which you can borrow from) tune in reruns of TV's long running *MASH* series and see "Hawkeye Pierce" in action. This character, deftly played by Alan Alda, picked up where Groucho left off.

Three types of humor that are fun to use

Twisting words and phrases

Mix things up occasionally. "You can lead a horse to water, but you can't make him gather moss." Or... "If you laid all the politicians in Washington D.C. end to end, they still couldn't reach a decision." Humorists Mark Russell and Norm Crosby are great at these.

Puns and double meanings

Groucho Marx was a guy who could fire off one joke right after another. "I just got back from Africa and safari so good. The first morning I got up and shot an elephant in my pajamas. Now how it got in my pajamas I'll never know! The next day I took pictures, of the native girls. But they weren't developed. So I'm going back again next year!" Oh, how about just one more? "Outside of a dog, a book is man's best friend. Inside of a dog, it's too dark to read!"

Snappy comebacks

Most of us appreciate a good comeback, but we always think of them about an hour too late. Bill Murray's character, named Phil Conners, in the movie *Groundhog Day* had a good one. A woman asked him, "Do you ever have déjà vu?" He replied, "Didn't you just ask me that?"

Don't walk on the laughter of your own jokes.

When doing a series of jokes, timing is important. After getting into a speech sprinkled with comic bits you will have a sense of how the audience is feeling and reacting. Hopefully they will be having a good time and laughing at the same things you think are funny. When this is happening do not cut off the laughs prematurely. If people are in stitches, which is every joke teller's dream, let them roll in the aisles for a few seconds. Don't make them stop just to listen to the next joke. It may or may not be as funny as the first one. When the laughter has almost died out, but not totally, hit them with the next funny line. But don't try to milk it too much, or your program may start to drag instead of picking up momentum.

You have to play with comedy to get the timing right. If things are clicking though, major laughs and a great time for all can result. By brightening an audience's day, you will go home with a tremendous sense of accomplishment.

Always think ahead.

Don Anderson, a veteran Toastmaster, once advised "Always have a story in your pocket." Now he didn't mean this literally. But his point was: you never know when you may be called upon to say a few words. The need may arise anytime for you to have to break the ice or fill up a moment or two of dead time during a meeting. So always think ahead to what you would like to say if given the chance.

Another piece of wisdom from Don: "Never say you are going to tell a joke." Don called his jokes "stories." His theory was that when you announce to an audience you are going to tell a joke, there is a natural expectation that it will be funny. So everyone expects a big laugh. If they don't get it, everyone is a little disappointed. But when you say you are going to tell a *story*, well, stories are not necessarily funny. So if you get a laugh, it is somewhat of a bonus.

One more tip—before telling a joke, <u>never</u> say to an audience, "This is the funniest thing I've ever heard in my life. You'll love it!" This raises expectations too high and you will bomb almost every time.

Humor can save a presentation.

From My Own Experience...

I was assisting at a public meeting one evening when one of the presenters had a moment of technical difficulty with a slide projector. We had to turn the lights back on so he could get the projector unjammed.

Audience members started shifting in their seats and I sensed we were losing them. Without missing a beat I blurted out, "So a horse walks into a bar, and the barkeep says, 'Hey, why the long face?' " This broke the audience up with laughter and they forgot they were about to get upset with a dumb machine. Immediately a young female coworker, who was also helping host the event, hit them with another joke, and they cracked up again. By the time the laughter died down from her joke the projector was fixed and we were on with the show.

Our little bit was totally unplanned and unrehearsed but it worked beautifully. After the program people filing out commented on what an enjoyable evening it had been. Some beautiful slides and two cornball jokes—it doesn't take much to satisfy people sometimes. And by the way, there was not one mention of the slide projector problem.

Humor can also turn a potentially embarrassing moment into a hit. A classic example of this was the night Johnny Carson's fly was down when he came out to do his monologue on the *Tonight Show*. (This of course predates Jay Leno's tenure as host.) Here was Johnny Carson, a big star, with his zipper down starting into a ten-minute bit. Television viewers wondered how he was going to gracefully get out of this one.

After a few moments the camera shot was slowly tightened up to where Johnny's lower half was no longer visible on the screen. The director then just held that tight shot on Johnny's upper half. Carson had not noticed anything wrong before, but you could see in his eyes as he glanced at the monitors that he was beginning to wonder why they were holding that same shot of him for so long with the same camera.

He began casting puzzled side-glances at the stage crew while still trying to focus on the delivery of his jokes. Finally, someone must have given him the "barn door is open" signal. He then just stared straight into the camera with a look on his face as if to say, "Oh shoot!" (Or something similar.)

Johnny then slowly and deliberately looked down at his fly, then gradually brought his eyes back up to stare into the camera again. Ever so casually he then slowly turned to face the back wall of the stage and did an exaggerated zip-up. Red-faced, but laughing as hard as anyone, he turned to face the audience. Everyone including the stage hands, camera crew and director howled with laughter. What could have been a disaster for someone else, Carson turned into huge success.

Anyone can be funny. If you have laughter in your heart and look for humor in whatever you do, you will find it. But don't be selfish by keeping it to yourself. **Share your humor with the rest of the world, so we can all laugh.**

— Chapter 14 —

Replace bad habits with good ones

◆◆

"Habit: A constant, often unconscious inclination to perform an act, acquired through frequent repetition."

— The American Heritage Dictionary

Some speeches are memorable for the wrong reasons. Most of us have at least a few nervous habits we have spent a lifetime acquiring. These tend to crop up when giving any kind of public presentation. While speaking though, we are usually blissfully unaware that we are doing anything to distract our listeners from our message. But very often we *are*. Sometimes subtle, sometimes not, these little habits can seriously affect the quality of our presentations.

Because we are usually oblivious to our own habitual idiosyncrasies, we may need assistance identifying and squashing these pests. The best way to do this is to arrange with a friend or coworker to carefully observe you while you are speaking. Have them pay close attention, not so much to what you are saying, but rather *how* you are saying it, and what you are doing physically. Make it clear that you want honest feedback because if they whitewash it and leave out things they noticed, just to avoid hurting your feelings, these problems will remain unknown to you. And of course, we can not deal with problems if we don't know they exist.

In college sociology we are introduced to a concept called "Johari's Window," which displays how knowledge about each of us can be broken into the following four categories:

1 Things you and others know about you. (Like the color of your car.)	**2 Things only *you* know about you.** (Like the color of your underwear today.)
3 Things *others* know about you, but you don't. (Like spinach in your teeth.)	**4 Things *no one*, including you, knows about you.** (Like an undetected disease.)

Bad speaking habits are usually in the third window, along with things like the "Kick Me" signs middle school boys tape to each other's backs. But by getting people to tell us about the spinach on our teeth, the sign on our back, and our bad speaking habits, we can move all of these annoyances into the first window where we can deal with them. Watching a video of yourself giving a presentation is a very revealing method of spotting some of your own problem areas that need work. If you happen to be hypersensitive to cameras and microphones, as most people are, study chapter 16 on interviews.

Let's look at some common examples of annoying speech habits we sometimes unknowingly inflict upon our audiences. Exploring these will help us see them in others and ultimately help us avoid them ourselves.

"Ums" and "Ahs"

These, and similar utterances, are called filler words. Most people use them in conversation as a momentary placeholder while piecing together a thought or thinking of a particular word with which to start their next sentence. To keep others from jumping in and talking at that moment we sometimes, uh, drag out an, uh, conversation by using meaningless sounds or, uh, phrases, uh, ya-know? It is rather tormenting to see these fillers in print and no less so to hear them in person, especially if someone has developed an extremely bad habit of it.

An excellent way to start breaking this cycle is to have a friend count the number of times you use filler words in a conversation or formal presentation. But don't shoot the messenger. Your friend may say, "It was an informative speech, but you used 25 uhs, 16 ahs, 11 ums and 5 ya-knows." As embarrassing as an accounting like this may be for you to hear, at least you will know the extent of the problem and can begin working on it. Just bear in mind that no matter how high the count, you are still normal and in no way beyond hope.

An important concept for a speaker to grasp is that *silence is okay*. We do not have to constantly emit sound during a presentation. In fact, silence can be used quite effectively to separate points, add emphasis, and give a speech dramatic flair. Another critical revelation is this: when giving a speech, unlike when engaged in a conversation, you do not have to be concerned that someone else is going to jump in and start talking if you pause for a moment. Why? Because *you* are in control of the audience. They are listening to what *you* have to say. So use silence to your advantage, and stop filling those brief voids with ums, ahs, ya-knows, duplicated words, and unnecessary conjunctions. Think of the act of speaking as though it were music. In any musical score there are rests strategically placed throughout the piece which gives it unique phrasing and character. Similarly, as a public speaker, it is essential to have brief rests built into your presentation style to separate certain words and phrases. Take care not to eliminate these important rests by inserting ums and ahs.

Jingling

People who carry change or keys in their pockets may nervously become what might be termed "jinglers." So before every presentation, make a good habit of always emptying your pockets of anything that can rattle, tinkle or otherwise make noise. This will eliminate any inadvertent jingling.

Hands in Pockets

Generally it is recommended that speakers not stuff their hands in their pockets while giving a presentation. Doing so limits gestures and may project a more casual appearance than intended. However, if you are telling a story where you want to appear very relaxed and informal, then go ahead and stuff away!

"Spider on a mirror"

Have you ever seen this? Sometimes, while focusing on their subject matter, a speaker will match up all of their fingertips of both hands (thumb to thumb, forefinger to forefinger, etc.) then repeatedly bring their fingers together and push them back out. It looks like a spider doing push-ups on a mirror. As a speaker, this may give you something to do to relieve tension, but while you are doing it, your hands are right out in front of you where they are clearly visible to your audience. Before long, some people start counting push-ups instead of focusing on what is being said.

Twirling a ring

It is always there on your finger and, if slightly loose, you may subconsciously push it up with your thumb a thousand times a day. When in front of an audience, and a bit nervous, you may find yourself messing with your ring just to give your hands something to do. But once you start twirling it around, the shiny object may mesmerize your audience. If you are hanging onto your ring, your hands will again be right out in front of you, so this habit will be highly visible to everyone as well as lessening your use of effective hand gestures.

Rubbing and wringing hands

Rubbing hands together back and forth can imply "Yum, yum. Let's eat!" Wringing them, as though washing under a faucet, can hint "I am really worried about this." Hands are expressive, and when we talk to people, our digits are right there between our listeners and us. So check occasionally on what your hands are up to, and make their actions appropriate for the occasion. Focus on adding meaningful gestures to your presentation style. Avoid just occupying your hands with annoying habits—the physical equivalent of um's and ah's.

Scratching

Being in the limelight sometimes causes us to perspire a bit. Oh let's face it—at times we'll sweat bullets! As pores begin to open they can feel itchy. Resist the temptation to scratch, wherever it is.

This is not only good advice for individuals, but groups on stage as well. Recently I watched several youth choirs perform and found a surefire way of drawing attention to yourself, even when surrounded by 100 other people who are all dressed exactly alike. While the rest of the choir is standing still on the risers with their arms at their sides, if you raise an arm up in mid-song and scratch the back of your head, you will most definitely be noticed—to the undoubted dismay of the choir director.

Whether singing or speaking in public, if the urge to scratch strikes, pretend you are in traction. Ignore the itch, and it will soon go away.

Tapping feet and bouncing legs

When called upon to be at a head table or part of a panel discussion, you are presented with the challenge of burning off excess energy discreetly. A tapping toe, bouncing knee or crossed leg flailing up and down will draw an audience's attention like cats to tuna. Now if you happen to be peddling footwear or stockings, this might be a crafty ploy to use. But for the rest of us, we probably don't want people staring at our feet or legs. At a head table there will generally be a modesty screen of some kind, such as a long tablecloth across the front of the table between you and the audience. However, there might not be. If you have anything to say about it, request one ahead of time. For panel discussions it is also possible that there will only be a row of chairs up front and no table at all. If you find yourself in this situation, check your feet and legs once in a while to make sure they are not doing the rumba without the rest of you.

Drumming fingers

This energy-burning exercise for nervous digits will shout to all, "I AM BORED!" Avoid it.

Yawning

This is a defense mechanism in response to nervousness for some people. With the stress of being in front of people, sometimes your body will seem to say, "Okay, I've had enough fun for one day, time to escape and go to sleep." A yawn may ensue right in the middle of a stressful situation. The unspoken message of course is, "Ho, hum. I wish I were somewhere else." Avoid this by being upbeat, keep your energy level high, and remember that your job as a speaker is to get other people enthused about what you are saying. Focus on *their* needs.

Looking off into space

Sometimes we will look off into space in search of a thought. To do this occasionally and very briefly is natural. But to fix your gaze somewhere and not maintain eye contact with listeners will give the impression that you are aloof and not interested in them. Or you could be sending an entirely different message. Like this example.

From My Own Experience...

It was a meeting of just three people, but it illustrates the point. A friend of mine went into a business meeting where he and a woman, whom he had not met before, were introduced to each other. This group of three sat down for a discussion. As they talked, my friend began to notice that the woman never looked him in the eye when she spoke. Instead she stared at the ceiling, the floor, at a wall or at the sky out the window. This was really starting to annoy him until suddenly it struck him. "My God!" he thought to himself, "This woman is blind!" For the next several minutes he couldn't concentrate on what was being said. He just kept thinking "Wow! What a courageous, intelligent person. She's gotten so far professionally without the benefit of eyesight." He shared this with me one day and we had a good laugh—because the fact is, she was not blind. She had 20/20 vision. She just had a habit of avoiding eye contact with strangers when she talked to them.

Draping yourself over the lectern

We discussed this earlier. Leaning heavily on something makes a person look tired. By standing erect and facing your audience you will appear alert and command more attention.

Turning away from the audience

If you have notes to refer to during a presentation, place them on a lectern or table in front of you if possible. This allows you to look down briefly then immediately regain eye contact without having to turn your whole body. Also if using visual aids like a flip chart, avoid turning too far away from your audience, and *resist the urge to talk to your visual aid*. Flip charts and blackboards cannot hear you, and neither can your audience if you talk away from them instead of toward them.

Flipping heads

Swishing hair back out of one's eyes over and over again is a habit many people find hard to break. If this is one of your challenges, try a hair clip, hair spray or haircut.

Looping hair behind the ears

Similar to above, this is a common problem for many people with long hair. Unless clipped or otherwise held back in some manner, long hair will fall in your face when you look down at notes. Even on Tony, Oscar and Emmy nights, professional entertainers can be seen pushing their hair back with both hands and looping it behind their ears a dozen times or more during a short acceptance speech. Faced with repetitive annoyances like this, many audience members will stop listening and start counting.

Pushing glasses up on your nose

Glasses can be tightened, and probably should be prior to doing a big speech. Nerves can, and usually will, cause perspiration. If your glasses are too loose, down they will slide over and over again.

If your glasses do slip down, avoid doing what a crusty old teacher at my alma mater used to do. He would always push his loose glasses back up with his middle finger. No one was ever sure if he was just oblivious to his habit, or if in fact this was a routine commentary on the profession of teaching, or perhaps our class in particular.

Playing with a pen

Sometimes we will pick up a pen or marker when we are speaking and forget to put it down. This can be a common problem when working with flip charts or whiteboards. Holding a pen or anything else in your hand for a long period of time, severely limits the gestures you can make. There are some people who seem unable to speak unless they have a pen in their hand, waving it around like a conductor's baton. The pen almost becomes a part of their persona, like George Burns' cigar. But stogies never got in the way of George's act; it was a part of the act. The speaker who always clings to a favorite pen risks distracting listeners from what is being said, with one notable exception.

Senator Bob Dole, a decorated war veteran who received serious wounds in World War II and served in the U.S. Senate for many years, always carries a pen in his less than fully functional right hand. He finds this a better alternative than having people wonder why he is shaking his fist at them during speeches, and it helps deter well-wishers from trying to shake his bad hand.

Excessive blinking

This is not a bad thing to do if caught in a dust storm. But blinking like a signal light on a ship will telegraph to an audience that you are very nervous. Remember that eyes are our most expressive feature and listeners want to see them. So let the audience see your eyes, instead of air-conditioning the room with your eyelashes. If you find yourself blinking more frequently to cover up for a tick in your eye, which may show up in stressful situations, you may want to see your doctor, just to be on the safe side. In general, you can calm your eyes by employing relaxation techniques, getting more sleep and exercise, and reducing your caffeine intake prior to giving a speech.

Checking your watch

Some of us look at our watches habitually. It doesn't necessarily mean anything, but people will often read things into our actions. How many times has the following happened to you? Someone sees you glance at your watch and then says, "Oh, I see you have to get going. Don't let me hold you up." If you have the urge to constantly check the time, consider placing your watch on the lectern during a speech. In this way you can check to see what time it is, or how much time you have left to speak, and the audience will simply assume you are looking at your notes.

Glancing at his watch was said to be one factor in the downfall of President George H.W. Bush in a presidential TV debate with Democratic challenger Bill Clinton prior to the 1992 election. The camera caught President Bush checking his watch. The impression it gave was that he was either bored with the questions or Clinton had him on the ropes, so he was ready to throw in the towel and get out of there. Granted, these were just perceptions the viewing audience attached to what they saw. He probably just wanted to know what time it was or how much time they had left in the debate. But alas, when in the public eye, perception *is* reality, or might as well be.

Constant throat clearing

Sometimes we experience a tickle in our throat while speaking. A glass of water will help and can also aid the occasional dry throat that gets raspy from too much talking. But if a tickle or cough mysteriously develops every time you start to speak in front of others, this is a symptom of excess nervousness. The very best cure for this is practice. So breathe deeply, relax, keep your pitcher of water close by, and look for every opportunity to stand up and practice speaking. This problem will eventually go away.

To sum up...

Don't let anything get in the way of your speech, including you. The more distractions there are, the less likely your message is going to get through to an audience. Remember, have a friend help you watch for bad habits like the ones discussed above as well as others which may be uniquely yours. (*Toastmasters* clubs are great for giving this kind of feedback on a regular basis.) And don't be frustrated if you find that as you eliminate one annoying habit, another one takes its place. This happens. Just keep asking friends for help in the form of honest feedback so you can continually improve your public speaking style. As you chase off your *bad* habits, *good* ones will eventually develop.

— *Chapter 15* —

Acquire impromptu speaking skills

◆◆

*"The ability to assemble one's thoughts
and to speak on the spur of the moment
is even more important, in some ways,
than the ability to speak only
after lengthy and laborious preparation."*

— Dale Carnegie

It is impressive to see someone stand up and speak eloquently to a room full of people with no apparent preparation time or notes. This is a skill most of us envy, few of us possess, but anyone can develop, by doing the following:

Live in the moment.

When engaged in a conversation, meeting or social interaction of any kind, focus only on what is going on right then and there. Be *in* the moment with the people around you. In this way you are going to know what has gone on and who has said what. When given an opportunity, you will then be able to respond in an intelligent, appropriate manner.

Believe in yourself.

Believe in your ideas and be confident that your thoughts are every bit as valid and important as the next person's.

Practice.

When an opportunity to speak off-the-cuff presents itself, dive in and do it. The worst thing that can happen is that someone may disagree with you. And don't worry that your unprepared remarks may sound "stupid." Be bold and act.

Listen carefully.

If your mind is wandering during a meeting you won't have a snowball's chance in a frying pan of being ready to enter a discussion. Have you ever heard something like this?   "Hey
_____." (Insert your name in the blank.) "You've been pretty quiet up until now. What are your thoughts on this subject?"

Oh man! Don't you hate it when that happens? Especially if you were thinking about your weekend plans instead of listening. To avoid embarrassment, and give yourself the best chance of having something intelligent to add to a meeting or conversation, become an *active listener*.

- Make eye contact with the speaker.
- Focus on what is being said.
- Show interest with an occasional head nod or other acknowledgment.

- Consider how you can best use the information the speaker is providing.
- Think about what more you would like to know concerning the topic that is being discussed.
- Take notes. This will help you stay alert and focused.

Form an opinion.

Everybody has opinions. If the boss or a committee wants to hear yours, do not disappoint them by holding back. Express yourself!

Expect to be called on.

It *will* happen some day, so just assume today is the day that someone is going to ask for your thoughts. Be ready for it. Have a brief speech waiting in the wings of your gray matter. Keep it simple, but try to include all of the elements of a successful speech—an opening line, one or two key points, and a closing comment. But don't agonize over it. Whenever you are in any kind of meeting or seminar just think of what you would say if asked to add to the discussion. What is it you would *like* to say? Make it short and sweet, professional and complete.

Here is an example: imagine being in a business meeting where a report has just been presented. The chairman looks around the table and asks for feedback. This is the point in many meetings when almost everyone will either glance at their watch, look at their calendar, or pretend to be writing something important.

A person who does not expect to be called upon in a meeting may be caught off guard and embarrassed if he or she has to admit that they were not listening or do not have an opinion worth sharing. The person who is an *active listener* and feels their opinions have value may look the chairman straight in the eye when called on and respond something like this—

"Thank you Madam Chairman. I agree with almost everything that has been said up to this point. However, I feel we need to place more emphasis on our East Coast marketing because of the downturn in numbers there. Jane's report on page 9 clearly indicates we are in good shape elsewhere. I recommend we go with Jane's suggestion for

upgrading our software so we can continue to increase our tracking and reporting efficiency. Lastly, I feel we should commend Jane for the terrific job she did on this report. It's very attractive and readable, and I think it is an excellent template for future reports. Thank you Jane."

While listening to others speak, be it at a company meeting, club gathering, seminar, banquet or other occasion, listen for items of interest which you may want to comment on later, if given the chance. Capture key words to which you may want to refer. A few scribbles, even on a cocktail napkin, will preserve your thoughts better than relying on memory alone.

During the business meeting above, shorthand notes that one might have taken, on which that 30-second speech was based, might look something like this:

Agree w/ most — w/ emphasis east low #s
Pg. 9 shows OK elsewhere GO w/ Jane rec.
w/ software for trk + rpt Udos, exH rpt
future Template. —

Prepare talks you may never give.

It is not always easy to guess when we may be called upon to say a few words. So if in doubt, be ready. Have a pen and note card or napkin in your pocket or purse, and jot down ideas as they come to you. Again, quoting one of the masters of public speaking, Dale Carnegie,

"Just as the airline pilot readies himself to act with cool precision in an emergency by continually posing to himself problems that could arise at any moment, the person who shines as an impromptu speaker prepares himself by making countless talks that are never given."

— *Chapter 16* —

Learn how to give a good interview

◆◆

"The only thing we have to fear is fear itself;
a nameless, unreasoning terror
which paralyzes needed effort."

— Franklin D. Roosevelt

If you are the least bit nervous about public speaking, you may be even more anxious at the thought of being interviewed. This goes double if the interviewer happens to possess a tape recorder, and triple if cameras are involved. But overcoming nervousness about being interviewed is just one more hurdle to clear in the public speaking arena.

The first step, which we will work on together in this chapter, is to get beyond the mystery of a formal interview. In the next few pages we will explore how the interview process works and what interviewers are likely to do with information they get from you.

The next step will be on your own. You must begin seeking out (or at least not ducking away from) opportunities to practice.

Reporters always seem a bit pushy don't they? That is probably because they are. There are good reasons for this though. Deadlines are one. There is a constant need in the news business to get a story out as rapidly as possible in order to "scoop" other reporters. Plus, reporters are often trying to talk to people who don't particularly want to talk. (Sounds like a good job in which to develop a quirky personality complex, doesn't it?) Most reporters are levelheaded, industrious people with a passion for covering the news. And they seem to get an adrenalin rush from being "on deadline," knowing there are only a few hours, minutes, or seconds left in which to finish their work.

To keep your adrenalin from skyrocketing the next time a reporter walks toward you, let us look at what they do and how you can work with them to accomplish objectives for both you and them.

Newspapers

Some day you may be part of a developing story that a newspaper reporter is assigned to cover. If this happens, you may get a call or visit at your home, place of work, or wherever the story is unfolding. The reporter begins with a self- introduction, names the newspaper being represented, and if in person probably hands you a business card. You are invariably asked, "Do you have time for a few questions?" If you have the time, are knowledgeable about the event, and are at liberty to speak about the situation, go ahead and talk. It will be good practice for you.

Talking with a reporter is not much different from chatting with your next door neighbor—except for the fact that virtually anything you say may wind up in the paper that evening or the next morning. But don't think about that. Just say what you know.

If a reporter is calling from the news office, you may hear computer keys clinking in the background since the story is usually roughed out as you talk. Knowing the reporter is typing while you are speaking can be a bit unnerving. If you want to help ensure that most of what you say is recorded and improve the chances of *accurate* reporting, stop talking occasionally and wait for the reporter to catch up. When you get an, "Uh huh" or they ask another question, you will know it is okay to continue.

All reporters are in search of quotable quotes. These are often referred to in the electronic media biz as "sound bites." They tend to be statements that are only a few seconds in length, have a ring to them, and will grab attention. The use of sound bites can oversimplify a story and may skew it in the wrong direction. But knowing that reporters are in search of these can be used to your advantage. If you have one or two points you definitely want to get across and you know a reporter will be calling, write them down. It is better to spend a little time up front and sound articulate than to be caught off guard, not knowing exactly what you want to say. And, a nice thing about being interviewed over the phone is that you can have all the notes you want laid out in front of you, and no one except you will know they are there.

On the other side of the sound bite coin, if you happen to say something cute or clever, no matter how newsworthy it is, you can almost bet it will show up in print whether you like it or not.

From My Own Experience...

As a public land manager, I was once interviewed over the phone about what vandals had done to a marshy area the night before. They had driven one or more four-wheel-drive vehicles into a wetland where they made a muddy mess out of what had been a pristine meadow of grasses and wildflowers. Waterfowl nests were ruined, wildlife habitat destroyed, and their tire ruts would be an ugly reminder of their stupidity for many years to come. I was not happy about this or the fact that vandalism of this nature occurred routinely in our area.

The reporter asked me, "What causes people to want to tear up beautiful places like this?"

My reply was, "I don't know. I guess it's just a mud-bog mentality." The moment those words left my lips I thought to myself, now there's a keeper. Sure enough, the next day my quote was in print.

If a reporter and photographer come out to the field together, you will be able to easily distinguish one from the other, for they use different tools. The reporter will have a pad and pen, the photographer will be lugging around a camera bag. They may act independently: the photographer running off to where the action is to get as many good shots of it as possible while the reporter starts asking questions and writing notes.

A unique feature of print media, compared to other forms of reporting, is in-depth coverage. Newspapers are not limited to a certain number of seconds of airtime per story as are electronic forms of media. But because newspapers only come out once or twice each day, (and sometimes only once each week for small local papers) they can not possibly compete with the instantaneous nature of radio or television, which can broadcast live from a late-breaking news story anywhere in the world. The paper, even if reporters are at the scene of a story as events unfold, obviously cannot get the news out to customers until the next edition is printed. Therefore, in-depth writing and excellent photographs are the strengths newspapers rely on.

Radio

Radio reporters operate in a world of immediacy. Many stations have news reports twice each hour, and announcers can always break into their regular programming at a moment's notice. So if a radio reporter contacts you, she or he may be putting together a story that the news director wants to broadcast within the hour or perhaps even the next few minutes. (Stories dealing with public safety issues such as accidents, fires and floods will generally be aired as soon as possible.)

When contacted by a radio reporter, you may be asked if it is okay to "roll tape" on you. This is a media term which means tape-record your conversation. Once the tape is rolling, even if the reporter already knows your name, you will usually be asked to restate your name. This is done so the station will have the correct pronunciation. It also provides a separation of stories on the tape for ease of editing.

Occasionally a reporter might like to put you on the air live via telephone. In this case, your interview will be broadcast immediately as it takes place. Live interviews will also be recorded at the station for subsequent broadcasts.

Radio is an auditory medium. Sound is radio's strength. So radio journalists want to capture voices of "real" people (like you) and sounds from the scene of a news event as it unfolds. This helps create mental images for radio listeners and adds more zest to a broadcast than simply relying on wire service "rip-and-read" stories which are generally told in the third person.

As an example of radio journalists' creativity—when covering a wildfire, good reporters will always get interviews from firefighters and other emergency personnel who are involved on the scene. But a very creative reporter will also get the sounds of flames crackling, bulldozers clanking, sirens wailing, aircraft engines roaring, and water hissing as it turns to steam when sprayed on the flames. The combination of good interviews and interesting background sounds make excellent radio stories. As the person being interviewed, you can help the reporter capture the essence of the story.

After gaining a little experience, whenever a reporter calls and asks, "Can I roll tape while we talk?" you will soon be able to confidently say, "Sure, no problem."

TIPS FOR RADIO INTERVIEWS

• When being interviewed for radio there will always be a microphone or tape recorder involved. Ignore it. That is to say, don't worry about it. It is only hardware. So relax and just focus on giving the reporter the information he or she needs for a good, accurate story. In this kind of speaking situation you have an audience of just *one* person. Concentrate on that person only, and your interview will come out fine.

Television

Facing a crowd through the lens of a television or video camera is a fearful experience for many people. However, with a little knowledge and practice you will not only be able to survive interacting with a TV reporter, but you will be able to give a quality interview.

As in any other speaking situation, when you are being interviewed for television, project as much confidence as you can muster. You are the "expert" on something, which is why a reporter has sought you out. So simply tell what you know as clearly and knowledgeably as you can.

During an interview, focus your attention on the reporter, and do not think about anyone who may view this tape at a later time—like the television audience. If you find it difficult to put the audience out of your mind, then think of them this way: they are individuals interested in what you have to say, and they are generally viewing their television sets only one or two people at a time while sitting in their homes. Therefore do as you would when speaking to a live audience; focus on providing these people usable information. Give them what they need.

News crews will always work with you to get the best video coverage and interviews possible. They will help set you at ease, thoroughly explain to you what they are doing and why, and tell you where to stand and where to look. They want to make you look good, which in turn makes their reporting appear professional and insightful.

TIPS FOR TV INTERVIEWS

- **Totally ignore the camera.** Pretend it does not exist. Look at the interviewer only—nowhere else—unless you are told ahead of time to do so. And never try to sneak a peek at the camera. It is still going to be there, and your peek will be preserved on tape. Reporters, on the other hand, will often look directly into the camera. But that is their job—to talk directly to the viewers. When you are in front of the lens, your job is to talk to the reporter. The cameraman then catches this interview on tape for the audience to view, as though they were standing nearby listening to a discussion between you and the reporter.

- **Plant your feet and do not move.** Once a camera is set on a tripod and focused, any shifting you make from side to side may put you totally out of the shot. The cameraman will not want to chase you throughout the interview. So remember, unless otherwise directed, stay still.

 - **Clasp your hands together.** Either in front of you or behind your back, put your hands together and leave them there. A television interview is generally not the place for gesturing. For one thing, gestures will not be seen if the camera-person is holding a tight shot of your face. Plus, gesturing will create

upper body movement, which will also move your head. This movement will be magnified on television. Once you start moving around you may inadvertently take a step and be out of the shot. So again, unless you are asked to move, stay as motionless as possible.

- **Microphones - Nothing to fear, just a little piece of hardware.** Generally, whether on the street, in an office, or in the studio, a TV crew will want to put a small lapel microphone on you to get the best sound recording possible. These microphones are only about an inch long, have a small alligator clip on them, and have a thin wire coming out the bottom. This wire will sometimes go directly to the video camera, or may be attached to a small transmitter that will be clipped on you.

  The crew will generally want their hardware to be as hidden as possible. So they will work with you to place the mike on your shirt, blouse, dress, tie, or jacket in such a way that the head of the mike is exposed, but the clip and wire are hidden. Hiding the wire, which is about three feet long on a "cordless" unit, is the trickiest part. Most often the wire is threaded under your clothes to the transmitter which can be hung on your belt or placed in a pocket. (Note—the crew will let *you* do any necessary threading.)

  Once the mike, wire and transmitter are set, the camera operator will do a quick sound check. To do this you will be requested to say something. It doesn't matter what. They just need to get a "level" on your voice. So you can count to ten, recite "Mary had a little lamb...," or whatever. And, just in case they forget to remind you, if anything rubs against the microphone during taping, (like a lapel, your hand or a piece of paper) it will be picked up as a fuzzy or scratchy sound. Minimizing your movements will reduce potential problems of this nature.

  - **Have key points in mind.** Before the camera starts rolling, know generally what you want to say. But do not attempt to have anything memorized verbatim. This would put an unnecessary amount of pressure on you. The reporter will always have several questions lined up in advance to ask you, and you will usually be told up front what these questions are, so you can be formulating answers in your head during the setup time. As with any other speaking opportunity, think of an interview as a speech (albeit a very short one) consisting of a brief opening statement, a few key points, and a concluding remark or two.

• **While you are being interviewed always try to work in the answer to the question you *wish* you had been asked.**

How the interview works

Once you are wired and standing where the news crew wants you, the reporter will stand either to the immediate right or left of the camera, which will generally, but not always, be on a tripod. There are times when the camera-person will simply hold the camera on a shoulder. This might be done for a very short off-the-cuff interview, and would most certainly be done for a walking interview wherein you and the reporter talk as you stroll along.

Behind the camera, the operator will be looking through the viewfinder and will be wearing a head set to monitor sound levels. After perhaps one last sound check the operator will indicate to the reporter that everything is ready to go. The reporter will then ask if you are ready. At this point you may be a little nervous, or perhaps more than a *little* nervous, but as Dr. Jeffers says, "feel the fear and do it anyway."

When everyone is ready the camera-person may say, "Rolling," or perhaps just point a finger at the reporter. The reporter will then ask you to state your name (or in the lingo of TV biz "slate" your name) and title if you have one. This part, as with radio, will not be aired but it helps the reporter get your name correct, and it separates the many stories a news crew may accumulate on a single videotape.

Once the camera is rolling and you are responding to questions, just think of the reporter as a friend or neighbor with whom you are having a conversation. Keep looking directly at the reporter, and remember, no sneaking peeks at the camera. As much as possible avoid those nasty little filler words like ums and ahs. If you need a moment to search your memory banks for a particular fact, word or phrase, opt for a short silent pause instead of a filler word. You will find that on tape, these short pauses are only half as long as you thought they were. And, if your pause is too long, the tape editor will probably just cut it out.

Generally, do not try to use notes. They will just be a distraction for you and the camera. Study up on your subject and what you want to say ahead of time. Try to imagine some of the questions you may be asked and practice how you might answer these. Then simply have faith in yourself to have a brief factual conversation with the reporter. If you are asked a question that you do not have an answer for, simply say so. Do not try to fake it.

During an interview if you suddenly realize that you just misspoke, and you would like to start over, then say something like, "Hold it. Wait a minute. I'm sorry, I gave you the wrong guy's name. Can we start over?" It is better to do this as soon as you realize that you made an error, than to ignore it and let incorrect information be broadcast.

Now if you are thinking that to start over is a big deal and a huge inconvenience for the news crew, don't worry about it. They do retakes all the time, sometimes shooting as many as eight or ten takes of a reporter doing a fifteen second trailer to tack onto the end of a story. So if they have to redo something only once or twice for you it is not a problem. Television crews are accustomed to interviewing people who are not accustomed to being interviewed. And, as was stated earlier, they want to make you look good so their broadcast will be viewed as professional and credible.

Before and during an interview always keep in the back of your mind what it is you would like the public to know about the news event you are involved in. This goes for any interview, not just those with television reporters.

Let us say you are in an official capacity on the scene of a ribbon-cutting dedication for a new Boys and Girls Club. You are very proud of the volunteer effort and donations that have come forth to help build this facility. But, you are extremely concerned with the fact that traffic speed in the area poses a serious threat to the safety of children who will be using the new center.

While being interviewed for television the reporter asks you questions like how much money was raised in volunteer donations, how many hours of volunteer labor was donated, and how many children will directly benefit from this effort. The subject of their story is not traffic. But, you can make traffic a part of their story.

When the reporter asks, "How many children will benefit from this new facility?" your answer might be, "We anticipate that seven days a week, 60 to 80 children will come through these doors. Most of these kids will be walking or riding their bicycles to the center. So for the safety of the children I would like to remind motorists that we all need to slow down and watch out for them. The kids are all so excited about this new center, they may not be watching for cars as much as they should be."

You see how it works? You do not have to wait for your question to be asked. Simply make the answer you want to give, part of the answer to another question. If it happens that you cannot get your key point woven into the middle of an interview like this, don't worry. You frequently have one more chance.

Often, the very last question asked by a reporter will be, "Is there anything else you would like to add?" This is the one question you want to be ready for, because if any of the key points you had in mind going into the interview did not come up, here is your chance to get them on tape. An open-ended question like this gives you the opportunity to free-wheel a bit. And, if what you say at this time turns out to be a great sound bite, you can bet it will be used.

From My Own Experience...

Several years ago I was interviewed by a TV reporter who was doing a story on motorized versus non-motorized recreational use of public lands. When the reporter asked that famous last question, "Do you have anything else you'd like to add?" I had an answer ready. I said, "One point I would like to get across to the recreating public is that we need to hear from people as to what their needs and wants are. We often hear only the opinions of outspoken special interest group representatives, but seldom do we hear from normal, everyday taxpaying recreationists, who are the primary users of national forests. But if the silent majority does not speak up for themselves, there is always a vocal minority who will speak for them."

Bingo! This last sentence was a sound bite the editor could not resist. The entire quote was left in and they ran it on the evening news followed by the reporter saying, "And, this next person may just be one of those vocal minorities." They then cut to a video clip of a red-faced, wild-eyed extremist who had challenged just about everything local public land mangers had tried to do in the previous few years. He ranted and raved in his interview and, in just a few seconds of airtime, supported my point beautifully!

The media can scare us sometimes because of the power it wields. But most reporters are professionals and take their craft of getting accurate news out to the people very seriously. So, if *you* have the best information available on a particular topic and would like to see it disseminated widely and in a hurry, there is no better way to do it than through the media.

If you are approached someday by a newspaper, radio or television reporter, just take a deep breath, relax, collect your thoughts, then seize the opportunity to tell them what you know.

One of the best pieces of advice on working with the media comes from Secretary of State (and retired General) Colin Powell. He said,

"You don't have to answer every question put to you. They get to pick the questions. But you get to pick the answers."[15]

Part Three

TO PREPARE QUALITY PRESENTATIONS...

— Chapter 17 —

Research why, who, where, when and what

◆◆

"Knowledge itself is power."

— Francis Bacon

When getting ready for any kind of formal presentation there are certain pieces of information you absolutely need. The more knowledge you have in advance, the more relaxed you are going to be when facing your audience. Plus, thorough research is going to make your speech more interesting, relevant and effective.

The Purpose

When asked to give a speech you need to clearly know *why*. If a college professor or your boss has assigned you to do so, that's a pretty good why. But what if someone else calls you out of the blue and wants a speaker? Before accepting any such blind dates, ask a few questions to find out what the expectations are. Do they need an informative speech on some topic in which you are an expert? Would they like to pay tribute to someone? Do they need help selling a product or idea? Do they want an after-dinner speaker to spin a few humorous yarns and brighten their day? Do they want a Master of Ceremonies? Or do they need a keynote speaker to open a meeting with a stirring presentation? No matter the reason, find out as soon as possible exactly what it is you are being asked to do.

After you know the purpose of the speaking engagement and have agreed to the task, begin gathering other pertinent information essential for a successful presentation.

The People

If you are not thoroughly familiar with an upcoming audience, find out as much as you can about them. This will help you tailor your talk to fit their needs. You would undoubtedly research a company before going for a job interview—so too should you research an organization before making a presentation to them.

Who are they? What do they want or need to hear from you? What are some of their views? What motivates them? What is the best way to grab and hold this particular audience's attention? How old are they? What is their gender makeup? Do they have a common educational background? What is some of the jargon they use? It may seem like a tall order to find out this kind of information. Here are a few ways to get the inside scoop on an audience:

Personal Contacts. The best way to gather information about an audience is to ask someone you know who is a part of the group. You might also make a list of others who may have facts about the organization or can at least put you in touch with someone who does.

Telephone. If you need to call an organization to get information, it is always best if you can ask to speak to a specific person. Even if that person is not in when you call, just by the mere action of using their name, others will be more receptive to helping you because you would have already established a bit of a link.

Libraries. A plethora of information exists in most public libraries about many organizations, both large and small. Reference librarians can help a great deal in this area. Two specific places to check are magazine articles and listings in *Who's Who*.

Internet. This powerful tool has information about thousands of companies, associations, societies, leagues, unions, clubs and individuals. If you have not yet learned how to do an Internet search, pay a visit to your local library or community college and ask for assistance. They will be glad to help you.

Arrive Early. Get a jump on everyone else and arrive at your speaking engagement early. And by early, I don't mean five minutes before you are supposed to speak. Get there an hour ahead of time. Or, if it is a multi-day event, like a convention, arrive the day before if you can. Give yourself as much time as possible to talk to individual audience members and briefly get to know a few of them on a more personal level. In doing so, you will be able to pick up a few names, inside jokes, and what some of the group's concerns are. Listen more than you talk. Have your antennae up and gather information that can later be woven into your speech, giving it a fresh, personal touch.

For example, you might say as part of your opener, "Your Club President was just telling me a few minutes ago about the kitchen fire you had here last month. This ties in perfectly with my topic today: *Fire Safety in the Home.*"

Perhaps one of the best reasons for arriving early is that the better you and your audience know each other, the more relaxed everyone will be during the speech. It's always nice to see a few familiar faces out in an audience. And the people in an audience are going to feel more connected to the speaker if they have had a chance to meet ahead of time and warm up to each other a bit.

The Place

Whether on your own turf, across town, or in another state or country, arrive early to examine and get acquainted with the space in which you will be speaking. Wander around. Check things out, and get a feel for it. Pay attention to seating, lighting and sound systems, and make sure you have answers to the following key questions:

- **What is the room layout?**
  Is it outdoors? In an auditorium? Boardroom? Classroom? Is there enough seating? Are chairs in straight rows or arranged in a fan shape? Are there aisles between the rows? These factors may be important, especially in large meeting halls when you plan to take questions from the audience. Give thought to how audience members will get to a microphone or have one passed to them before they start their question so that everyone in the room can hear what is being asked. This will keep you, or someone else, from having to repeat or paraphrase each question before it is answered. I am sure you have been to poorly run meetings where much of the audience can only hear answers from the speaker but can never hear the questions. Things like this are frustrating for listeners. So keep the audience in mind at all times and plan ahead for better meetings.

- **Where will you be speaking from?**

  Will there be a surface on which to set your notes? Will you be at a table, lectern or podium? Will there be risers or an elevated stage? Will you be free to roam around as you talk?

- **Where will you enter?**

  If this is a formal affair, it is good to know the route you will be taking through the halls and corridors to get where you need to be. This could help you avoid getting lost, tripping over a power cord or stumbling on a tricky step.

- **Is there a sound system?**

  If so, will a house technician be standing by to assist as needed?

- **What is the lighting like and where are the switches?**

  This is critical information if you are using audiovisual equipment. Are there dimmers or multiple switches, or will one switch plunge the room into total darkness?

- **Are there windows? Window shades?**

  Are there window shades to darken the room? Will windows need to be opened to allow fresh air in? If windows are opened will there be unacceptable distractions like street noise, wind blowing the shades, or odors, from say, a neighboring roof being tarred?

- **What is the room temperature and where is the thermostat?**

  A room that is too warm will put an audience to sleep. One that is too cold will have them fidgeting, rubbing their hands together and putting their coats on. Any space will warm up as people start occupying it with their warm bodies and constant breathing. So if in doubt, start with a cool room, but make arrangements to have the heat turned up if needed.

- **Is everything checked and ready for use?**

  For example, if there is a podium, is it sturdy? Or if you casually lean on it will it collapse and send you tumbling off the stage? (Hey, it happens. Senator Bob Dole in the

1996 Presidential Campaign can attest to that.) Is there a reading light? Does it work? What about visual aid equipment, like a slide projector? Does it work? Are your slides in the tray properly?

For your own piece of mind, double-check all of these kinds of things yourself. Don't depend upon someone else to do it because all too often, things are left undone. When President Bill Clinton was giving an address to Congress, he discovered his tele-prompter had been loaded with the wrong speech. If the President of the United States can't get good help, who can? We will examine visual aids much more in Chapter 21.

- **Is there a pitcher of drinking water and a glass available?**

   You never know when a tickle will strike or when your throat will become hoarse from talking.

- **Is everything you need present?**

   Do a mental run-through and see if anything comes up missing or is out of place. It is much easier to take care of needs and fix things *before* starting a presentation.

- **Who are your key contacts?**

   If you need something prior to or during the speech, who will get it for you? Have names, phone or pager numbers and locations of event helpers, janitorial staff, concierges, and others available to assist you. The last thing you want to have to say during a speech is: "This isn't working. Is there an electrician in the house?"

The Agenda

Know as much as possible about the schedule prior to arriving, but keep in mind that sometimes surprises happen. Other speakers can't make it. A piece of equipment breaks down. There may be a last minute change in meeting rooms. The best thing to do is stay as informed as possible to minimize these surprises. Some questions to get answers for include:

- **How many speakers are there?**

   If you are not the only speaker, and, if given a choice, volunteer to go *first*. It is usually to your advantage to be at, or near, the top of the speaking order. Your audience will be more attentive and less apt to fidget. After two or three speeches, even *if* the other speakers use no more than their allotted time, listener's minds (and eventually their bodies) will begin to wander off towards the bathroom, coffee urn, or the side door to stretch their legs and grab some fresh air. If you are to be one of the last speakers don't panic. Just realize that you are going to have to ramp up your energy level in order to hold the audience's attention.

- **Is this a dinner meeting?**

    At dinner meetings be prepared for the likelihood of clattering dishes and chitchat among diners and servers. ("Pssst! Excuse me. I ordered the chicken and my wife wanted her steak medium instead of rare.") If you want to assure a minimum of interruptions, arrange with meeting planners to begin your speech after dessert is served, and ask that no dishes be cleared until you are finished.

- **Is there a happy hour before your talk?**

    This could modify the attitude and attention span of your audience. It could also affect your performance if you join in the festivities. A good rule of thumb, no matter how well you think you can hold liquor, is to refrain from consuming any prior to a presentation. Once you have set this rule, it makes it easier to refuse a drink that someone may try to stick in your hand. You can simply say, "No thanks. I never touch a drop before a speech." Stick to your guns on this, because if you give in and have one with Jack, then Jill may want to buy you one, then Dick, then Jane. Eventually you could be the happiest person in the room, and be convinced that you are not only a rocket scientist, but a funny one at that. Your performance, however, could be miserable. So before ordering "tee more martoonies," stop and think about your audience and your reputation. Lastly, if you typically do not drink any alcohol, this is definitely <u>not</u> the time to start.

- **Will you be expected to eat with the group before giving your speech?**

    Some speakers do not do well on a full stomach. You be the judge as to whether or not to eat. Small portions are a good way to go. But, if there is something on the menu that you know will stir up a case of indigestion, do not eat it! (Even if your mother did teach you to clean up your plate.) You be in control.

The Subject

Nothing beats old-fashioned preparation. Even if you are an expert with over 20 years of experience in your field, do not assume you can pull together a meaningful presentation while in the car or on an airplane en route to a meeting. Your audience deserves more than that. Besides, who needs that kind of pressure? Invest the time necessary to do it right. Dig for information and assemble it in an interesting verbal package well ahead of time.

Start early, even if you have been meaning to join Procrastinators Anonymous but never got around to it. Whatever you do, fight the temptation to put off preparing a speech. The sooner you have some research under your belt and a few notes on paper, the sooner you can start relaxing. An added bonus for getting a quick start on writing a speech is that your subconscious will have that much more time to mull the information over. This will give your thoughts more clarity.

So make it easy on yourself. Begin preparing as soon as you can to avoid a last minute rush and panic. A key factor to avoid stage fright is *preparedness*!

Research and plan ahead for a successful program. For assistance, copy and use the Speaking Engagement Planning Sheet and other forms located in the Appendix.

— Chapter 18 —

Write from the heart

◆◆

"It is our attitude at the beginning of a difficult undertaking which, more than anything else, will determine its outcome."

— William James

Good speeches, like good speakers, do not just happen. Essential to both are the investment of time and effort. Abraham Lincoln once apologized to an audience saying he did not have time to write a short speech, so he would have to give a long one. Boiling down what you have to say into a concise, relevant package is more difficult than just rambling on about something.

Effortless appearing presentations take the most effort. Preparing a succinct and potent speech requires planning, writing, rewriting, organizing, reorganizing, and then more of the same. If you ever doubt that all of the preparation is worth it, just remember another speech given by President Lincoln, dedicating a new national cemetery during the Civil War. With words carefully chosen in advance, this most famous of American speeches came to be known as the "Gettysburg Address." Total delivery time was one minute and forty seconds.

Select a topic

Often the subject of a speech has very narrow parameters. If, for example, you are called upon to say a few words at a friend's retirement dinner, or Uncle Fred's funeral, you will want to stick closely to the subject and not stray too far into other topic areas. But sometimes your subject selection will be wide open. In an after-dinner speech you can usually talk on just about anything, as long as it is humorous. But no matter what the occasion or topic there is an expectation that you will put your own unique spin on the presentation. This is what makes speeches interesting. They are individualized and no two are ever exactly alike.

Start crafting your speech

Depending on your comfort level with a topic, you may want to initially write a speech out verbatim. Put down on paper all of the thoughts, comments and asides you think you may have time for. Then do a practice run-through to see how it sounds and how long it takes. You may want to do your practice presentations out-loud in front of a mirror, or you may just want to go over the material in your mind. Whichever method you choose, speech preparation calls for a quiet area where you will not be disturbed. Rework the material, add or subtract as needed, then try it again.

Focus

The attention span of an audience is only as long as the seat of the pants will endure. So no matter how charismatic a speaker you may be, there is only so much effective time available in which to say what needs to be said. A choice has to be made then. Will limited speaking time be used to cover many different aspects of a subject in a superficial way? Or, will fewer features of a topic be discussed in more depth? The latter is generally the better choice. For most of us, the connection between our short-term and long-term memories is, quite frankly, not that good. So if you want an audience to remember what you have said, focus your energy on a few key points and do them well.

Your primary focus as a speaker should be to prepare and deliver a speech that people will **listen to**, **remember**, and **act upon**. This is true no matter what your purpose in giving a speech—whether it be promoting social change, scientific advancement, teaching, improving the corporate bottom line, helping a friend transition into retirement, or a thousand other possibilities.

Make it you

All of us are most comfortable and convincing when discussing things that we know, things we have experienced, and events that have shaped our lives. So do your best to speak in true-to-life terms, instead of the abstract. Draw from your life, personalize it, and make it relevant to other people's lives. This will give a speech emotional punch. If you do all of these things, people *will* listen!

An audience can tell when you are talking about something you are passionate about because you will be more animated and spontaneous. So when writing a speech, and later when delivering it, take a little risk and pour your emotions into it as well as your thoughts.

Make it human

People are interested in other people—their ideas, reactions, what they do, where they come from. Audiences want to listen to interesting stories about fellow human beings. Dry terminology and facts will seldom hold attention or convince people to take action. So, each time you prepare a talk, ask yourself the following four questions:

1. What is the human element of this topic?
2. Why will people care?
3. Why is it important for them to listen?
4. What do I want them to do?

Let us say, for example, we have been asked to give a speech on the social and economic conditions of lower income families in this country. One could state the dry facts, which are:

- Over 36 million people in the U.S. live in poverty. Of those, 40% are children.

- 15 million people have incomes that are less than half of what is legally defined as "poverty."

- To afford a two-bedroom apartment, and still have enough money for the other necessities of life, a worker in this country, making the median minimum wage, would have to work 87 hours per week.

- Over 44 million Americans have no health care coverage.

- Each year in this country over 2 million people experience homelessness, a large percentage of these being children.

Those are the facts. But our minds become numb to these kinds of statistics. These numbers do not give us a mental picture that we can connect with emotionally.

From My Own Experience...

If I were asked to make such a presentation, I would draw upon my experience as a forest officer with the U.S. Forest Service for over 27 years. In that time I saw many unemployed families living in the National Forests. The approach I would take is to tell about parents I came in contact with, who, after having lost their jobs and homes, picked up their families and moved to a new area, hopeful of finding work. Too proud to take charity, they live in their cars or set up small tents in the forest and journey into town in search of work and food. I would ask my audience to visualize small children, often in ragged clothes and with few toys, who do not go to school, but instead live each day in the woods without enough to eat, without running water, bathing facilities, or even a toilet.

There are always stories behind the facts and figures. To be an effective speaker, find those stories and tell them. And if tears of sadness or joy come to your eyes as you write or deliver a speech, it is likely that your audience will experience the same emotions. When this happens you know they are listening and that you have connected with them. You have impacted their lives in at least a small way and you have planted a few seeds which may grow one day through the actions of your listeners.

Overcome writer's block

We have all experienced it. You sit there and just stare at a blank sheet of paper or computer screen, but the words won't come. Argh! It is the dreaded writer's block. Actually, this malady can be an excellent excuse to clean your closet, rearrange your kitchen shelves or wash the dog. Unfortunately, those things will not get you any closer to having a speech prepared.

One of the best ways to conquer writer's block is simply to write something. Write *anything*. Just get started. As thoughts come into your head put them down, even if they are only remotely connected to what you are working on. The mere act of moving your hands and fingers, or doing any other physical activity, has been shown to stimulate the creative right side of the brain. So the more you write, the more ideas will come to you.

The use of a personal computer is particularly beneficial for anyone who writes on a regular basis. The beauty of it is that thoughts can be put down as rapidly as you can type and in any order. Later you can easily go back and rearrange a random list into a logical outline form.

You never know when inspiration will strike. If you are working on one thing and suddenly ideas pop into your head about something else, capture them immediately! Thoughts are too fleeting to wait. Just drop to the next line and type the essence of your new thoughts. Do not be judgmental about them and do not worry about spelling, punctuation, or grammar. These are just rough notes, and no one else is going to see them. So don't be a perfectionist because if a thought gets away from you, it may never return.

Once ideas start flowing, get as many of them down as rapidly as you can. Resist the temptation to shut them off too soon just so you can go back and start tidying them up. Only after your creative juices slow from a gusher to a drip, should you then start to sort things into logical patterns, change spellings, fill in holes, create a new file name, etc. You will no doubt modify and rework this raw material numerous times. But that's good. It is by far the best way to write because you will be able to harness many more creative ideas faster than you ever would using any other method.

When working on a speech, or almost anything else requiring creativity, keep a pad and pencil nearby at all times. Keep these in your coat, your purse, your car, your fishing tackle box—anywhere from which you can retrieve them in an instant. The nightstand is an excellent place to have a pad and pencil because many thoughts will come to us as we begin to relax immediately before going to sleep. Sometimes too, an idea will gel in the middle of the night after the subconscious has had time to work on a problem for a few hours.

As mentioned above, physical movement will often stimulate a flow of creative thought. So, when working on a project, if your brain starts to feel dried up, go do something physical. Get your blood flowing to the brain. Take a walk. Go for a bike ride. Jog. Hit the gym. Get some fresh air. You will be able to come up with a much higher percentage of good ideas during or immediately after exercise.

The shower is also a great place to think. The heat, noise and water streaming down seems to temporarily shut out the rest of the world. It presents a good opportunity to consciously take on a problem for a few minutes with a higher than average degree of likelihood that a solution will present itself. But, before your ideas vaporize, remember to jot them down.

If you are still coming up short on ideas, try browsing in a library or bookstore. This can change your frame of reference, expose you to new ideas, and perhaps take you in a different direction than where previous thoughts were leading you.

The act of creating something from nothing is fascinating. Sometimes it can happen spontaneously with little effort while other times it can be a painfully arduous process. But keep after it. The reward of having people come up to you after an excellent presentation with words of thanks and congratulations make it all worthwhile.

There is an old bromide that advises "Well begun is half-done." This is not far off when it comes to preparing any kind of presentation. If you have a good topic and can come up with a good opening, you are well on your way.

*"Writing requires application
of a coat of glue
to the seat of the chair."*

— Anon

— Chapter 19 —

Organize your information

◆◆

"Good order is the foundation of all things."

— Edmund Burke

There are four basic elements of every good speech—an opening, transition, body, and conclusion. Organize your speeches in this manner and you will increase your chances for success.

The Opening

"I know of no more compelling method of opening a talk than by the use of a story," said the late Dale Carnegie, one of the world's foremost authorities on public speaking.[16] As we have already discussed, stories have impact. People will stop what they are doing and listen to a good story. As a matter of fact, people will go out of their way and even *pay* to hear stories. Look at the movie industry, video rental business, cable and satellite television, and live theater. Millions of people each day collectively spend tens of millions of dollars seeking out good stories.

Unfortunately, most public speakers do not hook their audience immediately with a good story. Instead, most will start off by saying something like, "Thank you for having me here this evening." They will then proceed to say, "Tonight I would like to talk to you about blah, blah, blah..." A form of this hackneyed opening is used all too often. Work hard to give *your* audience something new—something they have not heard before, and something they do not expect. This will keep them listening because they will not want to miss anything.

A surefire way of grabbing an audience's attention is to take Mr. Carnegie's advice and immediately begin your speeches with a short relevant story. Here's an example. Imagine you are in an audience where the welcoming applause for the speaker is just dying down and people are getting settled in. There is a moment of silence as the speaker gazes out over the crowd. Then he begins.

"The year was 1970. I was just nineteen years old. My squad and I lay face down in the dirt on an open ridge as large aircraft swept over the top of us. The thunder of their engines and payloads shook the ground while in the forest below there were continuous explosions and the constant sound of rotors as helicopters dropped incendiary devices.

Flames lashed at the tree tops and thick black smoke climbed into the sky.

Our radio crackled to life, and we were ordered to move out. As we trudged single-file down the ridge, we kept a watchful eye out for venomous snakes driven out of their hiding places by the spreading fire. We hoped there would be a good landing zone below for a helicopter to pick us up. Sweat streaked down our 20 grimy faces—the salt and soot stinging our eyes. None of us had been near a shower or a regular cooked meal for almost two weeks.

By sundown over 30,000 acres were scorched, and some equipment had been damaged, but everyone walked out of the woods under their own power with only minor scrapes and insect bites.

Except for going off to college the year before, this was my first time away from the family farm. It was also the first of many forest fires I would fight in my career with the U.S. Forest Service."

I was that nineteen-year-old kid and I can talk about this incident as though it happened yesterday because the memory is so vivid. You too have had experiences where sights, sounds and smells have permanently etched your mind. Whether battling a foreign enemy or a forest fire, or experiencing extreme joy, fear or sorrow—these are the kinds of experiences of which good stories are made. And we *all* have them.

The great thing is that once you begin telling one of these tales from your past, you no longer need a script, because you lived it, felt it, tasted it. Nothing beats firsthand experiences. This is what "make it you" in Chapter 18 refers to. When you open up and share yourself with an audience, you will captivate people and become known as an excellent public speaker.

The Transition

After you have captured your audience with an interesting opening, hang onto their attention while smoothly moving into the body of your speech. This is yet another opportunity for creating unique or humorous segues to keep listeners from mentally drifting away while you shift gears.

A rough example of a not-so-smooth transition would go something like this: "I'd like to make three points today. These will be: 1. Blah; 2. Blah, blah; and 3. Blah, blah, blah. Now as to point number one— Yadda, yadda, yadda..."

This type of transition comes from the school of "Tell them what you are going to tell them. Tell them. Then tell them what you told them." Speakers have used this method for a long time. In fact, it is how most of us were taught to make a speech in school, and it is still taught today.

But when you use this method, don't make the structure of your presentation so obvious by numbering everything. This will remind the audience that they are in fact listening to a speech and it may instantly shut down some minds in the audience as a form of rebellion—perhaps acquired from having endured too many less-than-enthusiastic speakers over the years.

Also do not give away too much of where you are going with your speech in the form of key points at the beginning. Later, when the audience hears these same points restated, their minds may start drifting off. Human brains do an incredible amount of high speed processing. So all of us have little tolerance for repetition and get bored easily. If a listener's mind has "been there and done that," it may simply move on to something else whether the speaker has moved on or not. You've been in many audiences before. Have you ever wished you could blurt out to a speaker, "You just said that" or "Tell me something I don't know."

As a speaker, keep things lively and interesting to minimize the mental wandering of your audience.

A better example of a transition might go something like this:

> While my buddies and I fought wildfires in the Western United States in the early 1970's, some of our old classmates were engaged in a much more deadly fight on foreign soil. As political winds shifted, our country's fighting in Southeast Asia finally ceased in 1975. Meanwhile, stateside, many of us continued to battle our old enemy of fire each summer.
>
> Unfortunately, because of its destructive force, fire has been villanized for so many years, that now most people believe

that any fire in the forest is bad. I would like to share with you today why this is not true and show you why we are now actually in a position of needing <u>more</u> fire in our forests and across our rangelands.

To do this we will look at a bit of fire history; Discuss how fire can actually benefit natural ecosystems and humans; And we will look at how scientists and public land managers are currently using low-intensity prescribed fire to protect forests and humans from catastrophic wildfire.

Notice how the opening and transition were used to set the audience up. They heard, through a personal account, how fighting fire has similarities to war. The old beliefs of fire being our enemy and "bad" were reinforced, right up until the second paragraph of the transition when they were jolted with the announcement that this is *not true*. They may have been shocked to hear a firefighter propose that we need *more* fire in our forests! With this kind of transition, listeners are going to sit up and pay attention because their interest is piqued. They now know you have a story to tell which they won't want to miss and you will have them wondering, "What's next?"

Openings and transitions are used to grab an audience's attention and prepare them to hear the main points of a speech. Once listeners are adequately primed and ready to listen, it is time to deliver the goods in the *Body* of your speech.

The Body

Earlier, under the heading of "Focus," it was suggested you pick out a few key points and cover them well. The body of a speech is where you will do that. Three to five points are as many as you should ever hope to have your audience absorb.

Each key point needs supporting information. Three to five sub-points for each main point will usually be about right depending upon the time you have available for your presentation. For most speeches, avoid assigning numbers to key points and sub-points and then using those numbers as you talk. It is excess verbiage and can get annoying. Imagine how it would sound if a speaker was continually saying something like, "And now we will move on to the fifth subpoint of my third key point." Let the organization of your presentation speak for itself.

To give the most successful presentations, tell a story—a colorful, descriptive story instead of a dry, lifeless presentation of facts. People like stories. They will listen to them and remember them. Facts and figures that are not somehow interlaced into an interesting tale can be easily forgotten.

In the following speech body watch how the three main points of fire history, the benefits of fire, and the use of prescribed fire are woven together.

Let's take a brief trip back in time. For over three centuries on the North American continent, European Americans and other new arrivals to the east coast expanded westward. As they moved west, these people did what had been done in their native cultures for centuries. They cleared trees, tilled the soil, planted crops, constructed permanent homes, built fences and barns for domestic livestock, and created villages and towns. But despite all of the clearing for buildings, roadways and agriculture, the wild forests and rangelands around them were still susceptible to fire.

What these emigrants did not realize is that before their arrival, much of this land had in fact burned every seven to ten years for thousands of years, because of the natural occurrence of lightning. If lightning did not start fires often enough, the indigenous people of North America would often purposefully set fires in order to maintain good grazing for wildlife and improve native crops such as huckleberries, roots, and mushrooms. The lifestyle of many Indian tribes allowed them to set these fires when they were ready to move on to other locations. When they came back to the burned areas, perhaps a year or more later, the grass would be lush, wild game plentiful, and food readily available.

However, this nomadic life and ancient land management technique did not match well with the European concept of land ownership. So, as Euro-Americans spread westward, they began suppressing all fires to protect their dwellings and other improvements they had constructed. Of course, they fervently discouraged the native practice of setting fire to forests and ranges.

Toward the end of the 19th Century and into the early part of the 20th Century many terrible large fires occurred that could not be stopped. Forests and towns went up in flames and people died. In 1905 a new federal agency, the U.S. Forest Service, came into being to protect and manage national forests.

But fire suppression techniques were still primitive and communications very poor. In late August, 1910, eighty-seven people lost their lives when flames engulfed three million acres of western Montana and Idaho. This was a defining year for the fledgling agency. Since then much of Forest Service history has revolved around efforts to find more efficient ways of rapidly getting to and suppressing fires while they are still small. The genesis of modern fire lookouts, airplane patrols, smoke jumpers, Smokey Bear, aerial retardant planes and more all grew out of those humble and sometimes tragic beginnings.

As the decades went by, fire managers became more efficient at keeping fires smaller and fewer in numbers, thereby sparing untold lives and property damage. However, in the latter 20th Century, a disturbing trend was noticed. Despite continuing efforts to stop them, fires were getting bigger and harder to control.

Close examination revealed that the cause of this problem was in fact what had been instituted earlier as the solution to wildfire. By suppressing all fires for several decades, natural fuels had been allowed to accumulate on the forest floor. Dead trees, limbs, needles, and brush had piled up to create a tremendous accumulation of natural fuel.

Over the top of this problem grew another one. Thin barked, heat-sensitive tree species, which had historically (and prehistorically) been kept in check by frequent, low-intensity fires, were now surviving and thriving in the absence of fire. These trees, which were not supposed to be there if nature had its way, added yet more tonnage of fuel to the forest.

Many of such species of trees, now growing outside of their historic range, produce a thick canopy of branches extending clear to the ground. Referred to by firefighters as "ladder fuels," they easily allow a ground-fire to climb into the crown of a tree and race to its top in a matter of seconds. Firefighters call this "torching."

If trees are growing very close together because they have not been thinned out either by fire or by humans, then when torching begins, it can set off a wild chain reaction known as a "crown fire." A crown fire can streak through the treetops, often with unimaginable speed and power—flames leaping into the air 200 to 300 feet or more. These fires will create their own wind, which draws oxygen from the edges of the fire to fan the flames even more. The wind and searing heat, often causing trees to explode, sounds like a freight train coming through the forest.

Human intolerance for wildfires and the actions we subsequently took to suppress them wound up making the forest fuels problem worse than it had been a century ago. In addition, putting out so many fires for so many years had other adverse impacts upon forest ecosystems.

By suppressing fires we unintentionally halted the processes of natural selection by low-intensity fire which thinned and pruned the trees in our forests . And now because these forests are unnaturally thick, when a fire does get out of control, the chances are much greater that it will be a high-intensity "stand-replacement" fire. That is, a fire in which most of the overstory is destroyed and the forest must start over from seedlings.

High-intensity fires can destroy everything their path, even severely damaging the soil on which the forest once grew. Without microorganisms in the top few inches of the soil, it sometimes takes decades for trees and many other plants to become reestablished. Without plant-cover for several years, soil is likely to erode off of hillsides and into streams.

This can in turn destroy whole fisheries for many years, by silting-in precious spawning gravels. Many fish species, such as trout and salmon, require clean gravel in which to lay their eggs. During incubation, fish eggs require a constant flow of fresh oxygenated water through loose clean gravel. But silt and mud stops this flow. Lack of oxygen causes the eggs to wither and die.

Without frequent low-intensity fires, trees become overcrowded, competing for limited sunlight, water and nutrients. Diseases such as needle blight and dwarf mistletoe, and forest insects like the tussock moth, spruce budworm, gypsy moth and mountain pine beetle can get out of control and reach epidemic levels. Slowly the trees in the forest die, creating even more fuel for subsequent fires. So you can see, frequent low-intensity fire can play a very important role in the maintenance of healthy ecosystems.

Knowing this, what can we do? Can we just let fires run wild through our forests and across our rangelands? No. There is too much fuel in the forest now and too much at stake. Large numbers of people, homes, cities, ranches, resorts, campgrounds, and other improvements are at risk. Unchecked high-intensity fires kill people, destroy structures, ravage forests and negatively impact soil, water, fish and other natural resources. Therefore, letting all wildfires run free across the landscape would be disastrous.

However, for several years now, scientists and land managers have recognized the problems associated with excluding fire from our forests and rangelands, and they have begun taking corrective actions in the form of mechanical treatments and prescribed fire.

Forestry research has shown that natural processes can be mimicked by a series of carefully planned and orchestrated human activities, which will not only protect the forest, as low-intensity ancient fires did, but also produce benefits for humans.

Logging can be used to thin a forest but in a less random way than nature. Excess wood fiber can be used for the production of lumber, paper and other essential products. Limbs, tops and other forest debris, which used to go up in smoke every few years, can now be ground up and sent to a cogeneration plant to produce electricity.

Once the hazard of dense forests with their huge accumulation of flammable debris has been reduced, land managers can then put fire back into these ecosystems through what is called "prescribed fire."

A prescribed fire is one which is planned and purposefully set, much as the indigenous North Americans did before the arrival of Euro-Americans. In writing a prescription for a fire, dozens of critical factors must be taken into account including such things as forest fuel type, tonnage per acre, fuel moisture, air temperature, humidity, wind speed and direction.

When an area comes "into prescription" it is ignited in a prearranged sequence to carefully move low-intensity fire through the area. The method of ignition will vary depending upon fuel conditions, accessibility, terrain and the objectives to be accomplished. Drip torches or fusees (similar to highway safety flares) are commonly used. Occasionally in larger areas, other methods may be employed such as incendiary grenades or other devices that can be dropped from helicopters. (Referring back to the opening of this presentation— incendiary grenades were the source of explosions my squad and I heard below us in the forest in 1970, as a backfire was set by helicopter to stop the advance of a large flaming front.)

A successful prescribed burn through a thinned forest will produce a light underburn, which will temporarily alter the appearance of the area. The base of many trees will be blackened, a few larger trees may have torched out and been killed, clumps of small trees will have burned, and much of the brush and grasses will be gone, but not for long.

Low-intensity fire areas recover rapidly. Within just days, grasses and forbs begin sprouting through the ashes. In a few weeks tree seedlings emerge from the soil. By the following year lush new forage is available for elk, deer, rabbits, and smaller animals. Trees that were killed by the fire will be inhabited by a variety of insects, providing food for many species of woodpeckers and other birds, which will take up residence. Within two years all scorched needles will have fallen to the ground. Five to ten years after the fire there will be little evidence to the casual observer that a fire ever occurred in this section of the forest. But the thinned nature of the forest, its consequent increased health, and the removal of many ground fuels will greatly protect this area from future wildfire.

This speech obviously covers several complex issues. A presentation like this would be greatly enhanced by incorporating a slide presentation to help illustrate terminology or features which may not be familiar to the audience.

Concluding Remarks

The summation of a speech needs to somehow wrap back around to where you started and remind the audience of the importance of your subject. A restatement of a few key items will hammer home your ideas and get your audience's brains to start transferring information from their short-term to long-term memories.

Never let a speech just end. People should not be left wondering, "Is that it?" Nor should they have to wonder, "What can I do with this information now that I have it?"

Most importantly, closing comments should be crafted in such a way that you modify audience behavior. It is like being a sales person and "closing the deal." You have given them valuable information and now before you let them go you can subtly (or not so subtly) ask them to do something with their new knowledge. This can be a call-to-action: You may ask them to write a supportive letter or contribute time or money to a cause. Maybe you want them to help recruit other supporters, or *do* more, *sell* more, or simply seek out additional information. Perhaps you just want them to help spread the word about something.

For the above "Fire" speech the idea was to develop an informed citizenry who will spread their knowledge among friends and neighbors. Here is the closing.

> *Fire—It is not all bad, nor is it all good. We need to suppress unplanned, potentially destructive fires. At the same time, we must aggressively work toward reducing forest fuel tonnage to reasonable levels through mechanical means. Only then can we safely reintroduce fire into many of these areas that have been devoid of it for over a century.*
>
> *Fire is a complex and controversial tool, but it is a necessary and natural element of healthy, balanced ecosystems.*
>
> *I think you now have a better appreciation for some of the many reasons why scientists advocate the use of prescribed fire in our forests. And I don't know if you realize it or not, but the knowledge you now possess on this topic is probably greater than that of 99% of the people in this country. I would like to close today by asking you to put this knowledge to good use by getting involved.*

If your community ever has a town hall type discussion about fire safety, forest management, or air pollution, please attend. Or if you hear of a land management agency taking public comments for an environmental assessment or prescribed burning plan, get in touch with them and give them your opinions. In short, please share what you have learned today with others and make your thoughts known so you can help shape the future of your forests, rangelands, and communities.

Are there any questions?

Question and Answer Sessions

Not all speeches will be followed up by a question and answer session. But, a Q&A period is a great way for both speaker and audience to squeeze more valuable information out of a presentation. Most audiences appreciate the opportunity to ask questions because it is impossible for a speaker to anticipate and then address in the body of a speech every question people might have on a given subject.

If you are going to have a Q&A session, discuss this ahead of time with the event organizer and set a deadline after which you will take no more questions. Some audience members would keep a speaker talking all night if allowed. So have a fairly firm cutoff time prearranged.

If you have additional time after the Q&A session, you could end by saying, "We need to wrap up our meeting now but if anyone has more questions I will be available for another half hour to discuss these individually with you." A side benefit of this technique is that you will be able to answer questions from those people who were not comfortable enough to stand up and speak in front of the larger group. (A situation many of us can obviously relate to.)

The best way to prepare for a question and answer session is to simply know your material well. Also, if an issue closely related to your subject were to appear in the news, you would be well advised to be familiar with that as well. Another way to prepare is to practice asking and answering questions of yourself. Write down some of the questions that you are likely to get from an audience. Go ahead and include a few potentially annoying or offensive ones to which you might need a gracious response. Then practice answering your own questions. You can do this while getting something else done that doesn't take a lot of brain power—like staightening up the house, washing dishes, or taking a walk or bike ride.

The thought of having to field questions bothers many speakers, sometimes more than giving a speech itself. It gets back to some of those old fears of personal interaction, embarrassment, or a feeling of just not being smart enough. Your little negative voice might kick in and ask, "What could I possibly know that these people don't?"

The answer is plenty! Only you have seen the world through your eyes. Your experiences and observations are unique. Therefore, those who listen to you will gain insights, which they did not have before.

Most importantly, don't be bothered by the fact that you may not have all of the answers. None of us ever do. When you don't have an answer to someone's question, an excellent response is, "I'm sorry. I don't know the answer to your question, but if you will write down your name and phone number I will be glad to find the answer and get it to you."

Armed with those few words, plus your knowledge and background, you can fearlessly face *any* question and answer session.

*"Have a handkerchief or tissue in your pocket.
The only thing worse than having to wipe your nose on
stage, is having to do it with your speech or sleeve!"*

—James W. Robinson

— Chapter 20 —

Make efficient notes

◆◆

"One of the secrets of life is to make stepping stones out of stumbling blocks."

— Jack Penn

Most presentations benefit from a speaking style that is natural, believable, understandable, and easy to listen to. To accomplish these characteristics, it is important to develop the ability to speak without a prepared script. Reading a speech aloud, while perhaps appropriate for a congressional inquiry, is inappropriate for the presentations most of us are asked to give. Speaking and reading generally have different rhythms which an audience will easily recognize. A minimum number of high quality notes will help you present a *speech* instead of an *essay*.

When you set about preparing notes, do not try to write down everything that you want to say. You may have already done this when you wrote out a draft of your speech. But now it is time to prepare an efficient guide to steer your speech in the direction you want to go.

Be selective. Pare down your written material. Zero in on keywords and phrases which you would like to keep in your notes. Go through these numerous times, continuously weeding out unnecessary verbiage. Your goal is a minimal outline, which contains only the true essentials you will need with you on the day of the speech. Your notes should be just mental cues, not complete sentences. The fewer notes you have, the more they will stand out when you refer to them.

The less dependent you are upon notes, the more natural and free flowing your talk will be, which will help keep the audience focused on what you are saying.

As Walter Anderson, author of *The Confidence Course* put it,

"If I read, you'll sleep; if I talk, you'll listen." [17]

Helpful hints on the use of notes:

- **Use note cards.** They fit inconspicuously in a pocket or palm.

- **Use large print.** It is easier to see.

- **Leave plenty of white space.** This will separate your thoughts and make them more readable as you glance at them. Plus you will have room to write in additional information as needed.

- **Highlight key words or phrases.** Colored highlighting or underlining can be used as a reminder to give added emphasis to a particular word, phrase, or idea.

- **Number cards or pages.** If your notes ever get mixed up, you will be glad you numbered them in advance.

- **Have a few spare cards.** Capture last minute thoughts as needed.

- **Avoid carrying your notes around.** If a lectern or table is available, leave your notes on it. Nervousness and shaky hands will be more visible to your audience if you are hanging onto your notes. This is especially true if notes are on full-sized sheets of paper. Also if you constantly hold your notes, or anything else for that matter, you will be unable to fully express yourself through the use of hand gestures.

- **Slide notes to one side.** When going to the next page or note card, be as inconspicuous as possible. When done with a page of notes, do not look directly at it as you move it. And do not flip it upside down to one side. Instead, after a quick glance down at the last note on the page, keep your eyes up while delivering your next thought. At that moment *slide* the used sheet to the side, creating a second stack. This maneuver can be done so smoothly that the audience will barely notice it, because you will be looking them in the eye while you do it. (An old magician's trick.) Anything you can do like this to make your notes less obvious will help hold the audience's attention.

- **Do not staple sheets of notes together at the corner.** Stapling forces you to pick your notes up from the lectern in plain view of the audience, thereby drawing attention to them as you flip to the next page. If you are using a microphone, the noise of this flipping action will be magnified.

- **With adequate practice you can rely less and less on notes.** Time and practice will give you the confidence you need.

— Chapter 21 —

Plan appropriate visual aids

◆◆

"I tell you and you forget. I show you and you remember. I involve you and you understand."

—Eric Butterworth

Many speakers use visual aids in presentations either because they think they should or because they want people looking at something else besides them. But unless you are working as a magician, a craft that depends upon creating diversions, resist the temptation to use visual aids simply to pull an audience's attention away from you. Use visual aids when they will provide structure, clarity, or additional information to an audience beyond what you can give them with your voice and gestures.

When using visual aids, never let them be the whole show. Bring the focus back to yourself frequently because a live person, interacting with an audience, is what will grab and hold people's attention. How long do you think people will stay focused once they realize a speaker is simply going to read what is on a handout or series of charts that the audience could read for themselves? They will probably start day dreaming or making weekend plans. So do not rely on visuals to do all of the heavy lifting in a presentation.

With that said, let us look at a few of the more popular types of visuals that can be used to enhance presentations.

Flip charts

The simplest and most available of all visual aids is the common flip chart. There is one in almost every meeting room in the world, and all that is needed to operate it are pens and readable penmanship. Flip charts are excellent tools for meeting spaces which are classroom size or smaller.

One common way of using a flip chart is to have key points written out ahead of time. Use pens that have a wide mark, about ¼ inch or more, and make your lettering large enough so people in the back row can read it. Be sure to leave plenty of white space between lines and along your margins. This improves readability and allows additional thoughts to be squeezed in as they come up during a meeting.

An old speaker's trick you can use is to write notes lightly in pencil along the side margins of your flip chart ahead of time. Standing close to the chart, you will be able to read these notes, but the audience will not. In this way, all the notes you need are in the proper order and in one place. You won't need a lectern, you won't need to turn back and forth from lectern to flip chart, and you won't need to glance down at notes. This will enable you to maintain better eye contact with the audience. Using this technique you can write whatever notes you need to for the audience to see, during the meeting. These can be written over the top of your lightly penciled notes if you wish. No one will notice, unless they are sitting within a few feet of you.

A variation of this technique is to write pencil notes for yourself on the back of your flip chart paper before your presentation. Standing to the side and a half step back of the chart, you can see the notes, but no one else will. Remember, while you are writing avoid speaking with your back to the audience or they will not be able to hear you.

Flip chart checklist:
- Paper
- Easel
- Different colored pens

Whiteboards and Chalkboards

Writing boards of this nature can be more effective in larger meeting spaces than flip charts if the boards are of a size that the lettering can be much bigger. Of course, as space is limited on such boards, there is the need to erase to make room for more information, once a board is full. If people are taking notes, be sure to ask if everyone is through copying before you erase. Audience members can get grouchy if you erase too soon, and there will be a momentary buzz in the room as people ask their neighbors what the last item or two was that they missed copying down.

Before a meeting starts, check to make sure you have the proper writing implements for the medium you are using. A whiteboard will be ruined by using permanent markers. And be sure you have a suitable eraser. Wiping off a board with your hand is messy and looks unprofessional.

Writing board checklist:
- Whiteboard or Chalkboard
- Different colored pens or chalk
- Eraser

Overhead Projectors

These can be used effectively in small rooms or big auditoriums. They are convenient in that transparencies can be prepared and organized ahead of time and photocopies can be made of this same information and provided to the audience. (See **"Handouts"** below for more on this topic.)

If you have several transparencies, number them and place them in a folder or notebook so they will not get out of order. In your speaker's notes, jot down the number of each transparency, perhaps in a bright color, in the location where you want to refer to that particular visual aid. This will help keep you organized. Even if you skip ahead in your speech, you can always go directly to the transparency you need, instead of flipping back and forth through them struggling to find the right one.

An overhead projector is a versatile visual aid system. It allows you to fully prepare material ahead of time, yet you can easily add details during your presentation by writing or drawing on the transparencies while the audience observes.

A few aspects of an overhead projector, to which a speaker must become accustomed through practice include:

- Use a piece of paper to reveal information on your transparencies one point at a time. If you have ten points on a sheet and allow the audience to see all of them at once, they will read all ten, rather than staying focused on the one you are referring to at the moment. Alternative to this, and perhaps even better—use ten transparencies with a single point on each one.

- Avoid looking directly into the bright light coming out of the projector lens. Your audience will disappear for a moment, and all you will see are spots before your eyes. If you need to point to something on the screen, resist going *to* the screen. When you look back to the audience from that location you will be looking directly into the light. Instead of pointing to the screen, simply point to the item on the transparency. In order to keep fingerprints off of transparencies, use a pen, pencil or other suitable pointer instead of your finger.

- Make sure people can see the screen. If it is too low, you and the overhead projector may block the audience's view. Check this out ahead of time. Generally the higher the screen the better. Also, as you talk, do not keep your feet planted in one spot near the projector. Move to the side so everyone has an opportunity to see the screen.

- When you want the audience to refocus on you, instead of the screen, either turn the projector off or cover up the glass with a piece of paper. If the projector is left on and is projecting anything, even just white light, people will tend to stare at it, expectantly awaiting the next slide or transparency.

Overhead Projector checklist:
- Projector
- Screen or white wall
- Transparencies
- Pens
- Piece of paper to cover glass and transparencies
- Extra Bulb
- Electrical cord(s)
- Table or projector stand

Tips for flip charts, writing boards and overhead projectors.

- **For each new point you record, alternate between two or more contrasting colors of pens.** This helps separate ideas from each other and they will be more readable from a distance.

- **A good way to get audience participation is to ask questions.** If participants' answers are then written down for everyone to see, it validates the importance of what that person said. This will draw additional responses from more people. Also the simple act of writing down answers will help focus the rest of the audience's attention away from the person who is speaking. This will put people more at ease and help everyone relax, open up, and respond to your questions. By using this technique you will be able to get some people to speak, who might otherwise have stayed silent.

Handouts

We often feel compelled to provide audiences with a detailed summary of what we talk about. We think we are doing them a favor because this will save them from having to take notes. If you are dealing with a complex topic or doing a briefing where it is imperative that everyone has the exact same information then yes, by all means, provide a handout.

But what do we immediately do upon receiving a handout? We read it! So, regardless of what a speaker may have to say for the next few minutes, the audience will be flipping pages, each person busily searching for what most interests him or her. We know this is true, because we *all* do it.

What else do audiences do if they have a very detailed outline or text of a speech? If the speaker makes any slight changes or omissions, even if done on purpose, people are going to notice because they will be following along on their handout. Of course there will always be someone who pipes up and says something like, "What about item 5c on page 4? You skipped that." They can drive you nuts!

When audience members are reading a handout, what does this do to the dynamic of a presentation? For one thing, people will naturally only partially listen to what you say. For another, eye contact becomes impossible. If people are looking at papers instead of you, it is just not possible to make the kind of personal connection with them that is necessary to have instantaneous feedback on how you are doing as a speaker. Without that connection, can you tell if they understand what you just said? Or has the information gone over their heads? Are they bored? Are you holding their attention? You know from the outset that holding their attention is going to be more difficult, because they are already diverted by reading and shuffling papers.

If audience members have their faces planted in a document they were just handed, do you think they will notice any attempt at nonverbal communication such as gestures or body movement? It's unlikely. So if you are thinking about handing out copies of a detailed outline or the complete text of a speech you are about to give, reconsider!

Unfortunately, many speakers distribute outlines, texts of their speeches, supporting documents and other reading material with the intent of distracting their audience. Some speakers will admit this, saying perhaps "I don't want everyone looking at me all at once. So if I can give them something to read, I won't feel so nervous." But is this the best thing for the audience? Providing them with a distracting handout? No. Will this help the speaker effectively connect and communicate with the group? No. Does this focus on the audience's needs? No. If this is *your* habit, then begin to wean yourself from reliance on handouts designed to distract the audience from you.

As stated above, if you have a complex topic and the audience must have a handout to fully understand the material, then by all means give them one. But do it at an appropriate time. One option is to withhold the handout for a while and say something like, "I want to talk about this concept for a few minutes and then I will give you a handout. But for right now, please don't take any notes, just listen."

Do you see the difference? In telling the audience they are going to get a handout, they are freed from the drudgery of trying to capture everything on paper that you are saying. By withholding the document temporarily and specifically asking the audience to listen, you will get their immediate attention. During this time you can hook their interest by using eye contact, gestures, body movement and all the other techniques we have talked about up to this point. (Of course, we all know some rather tightly wound people who will take notes no matter what they are told. Oh well. Let them do their thing.)

Audio/Visual Equipment

Data, graphs, illustrations and photographs can be easily and efficiently shared with audiences through electronic means these days. Back in the 1950's and 60's "audio/visual equipment" meant bulky filmstrip projectors, complicated and frustrating reel-to-reel movie projectors, and overhead projectors so massive they approached the size of major household appliances. Thankfully, equipment today is more compact and easier to use.

As you organize a presentation keep in mind that most people's lives are now busier than ever before. It seems we are all trying to cram twenty-five hours into a twenty-four hour day by using E-mail, answering machines, cell phones, laptop computers, fax machines, pagers, scanners, digital cameras, wireless Internet and more. With this frenzy of activity going on, audiences become distracted easily, and they simply will not sit still for anything that does not hold their attention.

So if you are planning to dim the lights for an electronic audio/visual presentation, be prepared to give your audience energy, variety and pizzazz. If you don't, the crowd may be smaller when the lights are turned back up. (Be honest, when was the last time you ducked out of a "snoozer" presentation so you could get something more productive done?)

Today's arsenal of audio/visual (AV) equipment includes some of the "older" technology such as overhead projectors (much smaller today than in yesteryear), slide projectors and video players. But there is a whole raft of modern AV hardware available including laptop computers that can be linked to image projectors, telecommunications equipment for audio and video conferencing, and more. AV technology is changing daily.

A very popular electronic presentation program in use today is Microsoft *PowerPoint*. It can help anyone make beautiful animated or still presentations with matching handouts. You can allow your imagination free rein with colors, clipart, imported documents, graphics, and font types and sizes. There are standard templates you can choose from or you can design your own. If you have not yet seen this tool, which is part of the Microsoft Office package, ask to try it at your local library, community college, business center or computer store.

One thing that all electronic gadgets have in common is the ability to not work when you flip the "ON" switch. For this reason *always* have a back-up plan. It may not be nearly as good as your original planned presentation, but it will undoubtedly be better than nothing—which is what you will have without a back-up plan. Many times each day, somewhere in the world, there are speakers whose laptops will not boot-up at the beginning of their presentation or (horror of horrors) they grabbed the wrong CD or diskette, leaving the one they really need many miles away. When you are preparing an electronic presentation, ask yourself what you will do if it does not work. Once you have answered this question, you will be able to confidently proceed on speech day, knowing that you can handle anything that comes your way.

And if something does go wrong—don't apologize excessively or express endless regret about not having the originally planned presentation. This makes both you and the audience agree that your work was less than adequate. Just initiate your back-up plan and give them the best that you have. After all, they came to see and hear a live person—*you*, not just some visual aids. You are the star. Your visual aids are the supporting cast.

Tips for using AV equipment:

- Double check everything. Leave nothing to chance.
- Practice ahead of time so you know that everything works.

- Have extra bulbs, cords, and batteries. (Better to have too many than too few.)

- Know which buttons to push and in what sequence.

- Know the location of switches and outlets (and know which controls what.)

- Arrange for a helper to handle details of lights, etc.

- Have a penlight with you. (Good for finding switches in the dark.)

- Delegate whenever possible, but do not assume anything. Follow up. Ask helpers before going on, "Do we need anything? Are we all set?"

- Have a back up plan. In case your VCR goes down have a replacement close at hand or a flip chart to write on. (Surviving and thriving in the face of adversity is the sign of a champion. Being doubly prepared to succeed can almost guarantee an outstanding performance.)

- Remember to talk to the audience, not your visual aid.

From My Own Experience...

Here is an example of how not to communicate with your helper when doing a slide presentation. One evening I was scheduled to help a coworker show a slide-tape program to more than 200 people. I arrived early to set up. The screen was placed so everyone could see it. Projectors, speakers, tape player and lap-dissolve unit were all wired together and tested. Slide overlap, focus and sound were all set. A complete run-through was done to ensure everything would run properly. The slide trays were reset to their starting positions, and the sound tape was rewound. I arranged for a helper to turn off the house lights when we reached a pre-designated point in the program, at which time I would start the show.

The evening was kicked off by the emcee. A couple of speeches were given and I was soon to find out that my lightman was a real "Johnny-on-the-spot." At the precise instant the agreed upon cue words were spoken, bam! The room was plunged into total darkness.

Hmmm. This is not exactly how I had envisioned things going. What I had planned (but unfortunately failed to mention to my helper) was that he and I would make eye contact at that point in the speech and then, perhaps after a nod of my head, he would turn out the lights. But that is not, of course, what happened.

So, there we were in the dark. "No problem," I thought. I only had to flick two switches and push one button. Hmmm. BIG problem! The room was so dark I could not see, and I didn't want to risk fouling up any of the settings I had already made on the equipment. So after an embarrassed moment of darkened silence, everyone heard me say, "Excuse me. Could you turn the lights back on for a second please?"

Once I got the machines turned on, the program ran without a hitch. But it could have proceeded smoothly without any interruption, if I had simply communicated more clearly with my helper.

Props

Physical objects can be important visual aids for salespeople, teachers, instructors, trainers or anyone who needs to demonstrate something. If a picture is worth a thousand words, then the ability to show an audience a real object and how it works is worth even more.

Imagine trying to sell products without having them to show to potential buyers; or trying to teach people a new computer program without having software to work with; or teach golf without golf clubs. And how effective do you think a Martha Stewart or "Galloping Gourmet" demonstration would be without anything for the audience to view?

Props are important. They show what objects look like and help us nonverbally explain how they work. What this means to you as a presenter is that you don't have to work so hard. You can use fewer words and let the object speak more for itself. So use physical props as often as you can.

The two most important elements of using props are:

1. Be intimately familiar with the object.
Imagine the impression a car salesman would leave if he couldn't find the latch to open the hood to show you the engine.

2. Be prepared. Practice before a presentation.
The Boy Scout motto, "Be Prepared," should also be the speaker's motto, especially when it comes to props because if something can go wrong, it just might.

 *From My Own Experience...*

When I was in high school speech class, we were given an assignment to bring something from home we could use in a demonstration/sales speech. One kid brought his new transistor radio – the 1966 version of a "boom box." He gave a nice little sales pitch wherein he told us how much power it had, how many transistors, what size the speakers were, how much it cost and so forth. Then he extended the antenna and turned it on to give us a sample of its sound quality.

After the demonstration he turned the radio off and said, "In conclusion, I'd like to say this is a good sturdy radio, and I highly recommend you buy one. Thank you."

With that, he put the palm of his hand on top of the radio's two-foot long antenna and shoved down, immediately bending the aerial in half! The class got a big laugh out of it, he got his pride hurt, and then he had to buy a new antenna. Thank goodness he was not giving a professional sales pitch, on which his livelihood depended.

Summing up Visual Aids

When planning to use visual aids familiarize yourself with everything about them. Make sure you have everything you need. Know how things work, and check to see that they do. And just because something was okay yesterday, does <u>not</u> mean it is still okay today. Do a run-through. Coordinate well with others, and leave little to chance.

There is an old carpenter's saying, "Measure twice, cut once." This avoids a waste of time and lumber. In order to avoid wasting time and credibility, check your visual aids twice.

It has been estimated that up to 87% of the information that we gather is via sight, 7% through hearing, and 6% through our other senses.

Part Four

TO ACHIEVE YOUR SPEAKING GOALS...

— *Chapter 22* —

Seek multiple sources of wisdom

◆◆

*"Wisdom is knowing what to do next;
virtue is doing it."*

— David Starr Jordan

The more sources of information and training you expose yourself to, the faster you will progress toward your goal. If you have not yet done so, take advantage of some of the following opportunities to gain additional information, assistance, and personalized help.

Toastmasters International

Mentioned earlier, one of the best organizations to help you overcome excessive nervousness and become a better speaker is Toastmasters International. This is "a non-profit educational organization of clubs throughout the world dedicated to teaching skills in public speaking and leadership." Here is a place where you are given an opportunity to learn and practice presentation skills every week. Check the phone book for a club near you. There are over 8900 clubs worldwide. Or you can phone the main office at 1-800-9WE-SPEAK; e-mail: clubs@toastmasters.org; or send regular mail to Toastmasters International, P.O. Box 9052 Mission Viejo, Ca 92690-1207.

Dale Carnegie

Helpful seminars, courses, corporate solutions and coaches are available from this company of long-standing. You may contact them via the Internet at www.dalecarnegie.com. Not only do they provide training in communications and public speaking but also in numerous other areas such as defining goals, setting priorities, increasing productivity, stress, mentoring, executive development, leadership skills and more.

Written Materials

Libraries and bookstores are of course wonderful sources of information. Supplemental to these we now have the Internet, which is fantastic for research. With it you can rapidly find books, magazine articles, and scientific papers on almost every topic. There are literally millions of pieces of information on the web, and it is updated daily with knowledge from throughout the world.

The best advice I can give you is to log on to the web. If you do not yet have an understanding about how this technology works, then go to your nearest public library, high school, college computer facility or computer store. They will be glad to help you get started. Don't catch yourself saying, "No, I couldn't do that. You can't teach old dogs new tricks." My siblings and I chipped in to buy our parents their first computer when our father was 80 years young and our mother 75. They learned how to surf the net and send e-mails, and you can too!

Once on-line, you will find a plethora of information. The other day I did a search using the phrase "fear of public speaking" and it brought up over 140 sites; many of these have multiple links to numerous other exciting sites. So boot-up, log on, and enjoy the research. But be careful to not fall into the trap of just reading about how to change or improve. Eventually you are going to have to log off of the computer or put down your book and get on with accomplishing your goals. Reading can expand your knowledge base, but *doing* is how you will make real progress.

Seminars

You can find out about worthwhile seminars through your place of work, chambers of commerce, Small Business Development Centers, Toastmasters clubs, speakers associations, community colleges, universities, professional societies and trade groups.

Seminars can be custom tailored for any size group or company. A good example is a one-day session I attended several years ago, sponsored by our local speakers association. A professional voice coach spoke to us. He then observed and videotaped each speaker giving a sample speech, after which he gave us individualized feedback and instruction in front of the whole group so everyone could learn from each other's mistakes. It made for an intense but very worthwhile Saturday. In fact, two of the people he coached that day would probably say that they experienced a "significant life event" during the session, for he helped them see improvements they could make in their speaking styles which they had each been overlooking for years.

Private coaches

It is surprising how many of us are able to get along for years without getting caught in a crisis. But the day we have to admit to ourselves, and perhaps the rest of the world, that we have a problem with stage fright, is the day we wish we had done something about it before. Trainers are frequently called in at the last minute to rescue those who waited too long and suddenly feel trapped by an upcoming major presentation.

Private coaches are able to identify and help solve problems that lead to stress and anxiety if left unchecked. They can tailor a program to concentrate on specific needs of a client— presentation style, microphones, cameras, media interviews, or other areas in need of practice and polish. Some coaches will even help craft speeches.

So if you or someone you know has the presentation of a lifetime coming up, are not yet ready for it, and are perhaps a bit panicky about it—a private coach may be the way to go. To reduce anxiety on everyone's part though, seek help in a timely manner. The sooner you get someone working with you, the sooner you will be able to relax. Information on coaches in your area may be obtained through speaker's associations, chambers of commerce, professional societies, or Toastmasters International.

— Chapter 23 —

Employ a formula for success

◆◆

*"In order to succeed,
you have to have a made up mind."*

— Cathy Benedeto
Women's College Basketball Coach

To assist you in improving your public speaking skills, here is a seven-step formula that only the most highly productive peak-performers put to use. Many people have heard or read this kind of information before, but only those who are motivated and truly want to succeed will follow through with all of the steps.

If someone were to ask, "What is important to you? What gets you motivated?", would you have any answers?

Sometimes we cruise through life more or less just waiting for stuff to happen. And sure enough, it does. But is it what we want? Someone once said, "If you don't know where you are going, any road will take you there." To help make sure you are going down the right road, and in the direction you want to travel, here are a few tips.

1. Decide exactly what you want.

Take the time to think about and set very specific goals. Goals are like a road map to help you get where you want to be. Without them you may wander all over the place.

2. Write it down.

It seems only logical to preserve on paper what you have put effort into thinking about. The most faded ink is more reliable than the very best memory. So write your goals down. Preserve your map.

3. Prioritize.

What is the most important goal you have? What's second? Third? Revisit this priority list often and revise it as necessary. As we change, so do our goals and priorities.

4. List steps needed to achieve your goals.

We cannot simply say, "I want a better job" or "I want more satisfaction out of life" or "I want to be a better public speaker." Then all of a sudden PRESTO! Things magically happen. We need a plan with specific steps outlined.

For example, if you want a different career, you may make a list of steps that include the following:

- Research the qualifications for positions in the career field that interests me.

- Set up an appointment, and interview someone currently in that field.

- Ask about training opportunities that will provide me necessary skills.

- Talk to friends and relatives who may have connections in the business.

5. Set specific deadlines.

How long does it take to get something done? When there are no timelines attached, it could be never.

Let's say you take a wristwatch in for repair, but you and the jeweler fail to discuss a date or time when you can pick it up. How would either of you know what the expectations were? And would the repair job *ever* get done? To assure that it does, we usually have some kind of verbal agreement.

We all know that our "I'll get to it someday" lists rarely get done. So make a contract with yourself, set deadlines, and hold yourself accountable to meet them.

6. Every day, do something toward achieving a major goal.

It does not have to be a huge item, but force yourself each day to do at least one thing that will move you closer toward one of your goals. It could be as simple as making a phone call, reading a magazine article, writing a to-do list, or sending an e-mail message. But do something. Rome wasn't built in a day, but you can bet someone was working on it *every* day.

7. Focus

A little-discussed fact is that successful people think about what they want most of the time. So review your goals often and, at least once a day, think about what you want. Visualize, as specifically as you can, exactly what you want to achieve, what you want to overcome, what you want to be, how you want to live, the kind of memories you want to create, or the accomplishments you would like to be remembered for.

We humans have an infinite capacity to change and become better at whatever we choose to focus on. Nothing external controls us as much as we control our own lives through our spirit, beliefs, and actions. Each of us must simply decide what it is we want, then seize every opportunity that comes our way to move in that direction. If you follow the seven-step formula outlined above, you will be successful in whatever you choose to do—no question about it.

Simple, humble people can move mountains if they are willing to think and act beyond what they already know and what is comfortable to them. As the famous entrepreneur and success coach Napoleon Hill stated more than a half century ago...

> **"If you can conceive it, and believe it,
> you can achieve it!"**

— *Chapter 24* —

Learn to believe

◆◆

"Whether you think you can or can't, you're right."

— Henry Ford

The fear of self-expression is a powerful force—so powerful, it holds many people in its vice-like grip their entire lives. They cannot escape because they *believe* they cannot. This is not unlike a horse, trained to fear the sting of an electric fence. Although large and strong, a horse can be held inside a corral with a single strand of cotton string which would be incapable of restraining even a charging mouse. The horse, however, thinking the string is an electric wire, will stand behind the string all day long because he has come to believe that escape is impossible.

As rational human beings we can break the imaginary barriers that hold us back. We can escape the clutches of fear. But first, we must *believe* that we can, believe in our selves, and believe we are strong, capable, and can do anything we set our minds to.

In a holiday movie, *The Santa Clause*, Tim Allen is surprised to find himself at the North Pole, replacing the previous Saint Nick, who met an untimely demise falling from Tim's slippery roof. While standing in a magnificent subterranean toyshop filled with busy elves the skeptical Tim cannot believe what he is seeing. An elf named Judy tries to help him understand. "Seeing isn't believing," she said. "Believing is seeing. Kids don't have to see this place to know it exists. They just know in their hearts that it does."

Believing *is* seeing. As you begin to believe in success, you will see yourself being successful. As you move from one achievement to another and another, you will eventually realize that success is <u>not</u> some far away destination. Rather it is an accumulation of what you do each day of your life.

It is astounding to consider the vast potential for achievement that lies dormant within each of us. While it is true that many of us are shy and afraid to reach for our dreams and express ourselves openly, it is also a fact that we can change. If we are willing to take a chance and invest some effort, we can make those first tentative steps toward our dreams and toward success. After that, each step becomes easier.

Controlling shyness and stage fright is about more than standing up in front of audiences and making presentations. It is about taking control of your life. It is about expressing who you are, what you like, and what you do not like. It is about overcoming the fear of saying what you think about personal or social issues. It is about being free from that little voice inside that may have told you for years that you are not good enough and that you can't change.

My friends, you *are* good enough, and you *can* change the way you view the world and the way the world views you. You *can* eliminate your fear, tear down your self-imposed mental barriers, and realize your dreams! Just remember, on your journey through life, each step you take is part of your success. Celebrate your successes, both large and small.

"When one advances confidently
in the direction of his dreams and endeavors
to live the life that he has imagined,
he will meet with great success
- unexpected in common hours."

— Henry David Thoreau

Still can't speak?
Don't give up – get help.

Fear grips some people tighter than others. There's nothing wrong with that. It is just reality. So, after having read this book and tried its advice, if you are still having trouble getting beyond your fear, I would like to suggest that you read Dr. John Marshall's book <u>SOCIAL PHOBIA – From Shyness to Stage Fright</u> (ISBN 0-465-07214-3). His book provides case studies and information about the diagnosis and treatment of social phobia. He also discusses several other common anxiety disorders.

It could be that your situation calls for professional treatment, which may include pharmacological assistance. If you do need this level of help, don't be embarrassed by it and don't put it off. We cannot always solve our own problems. Sometimes we need help. So just ask for it. The sooner you do, the sooner you will be able to move beyond your fear and fulfill your dreams.

Pick up the phone, pay a personal visit, write a letter, or send an e-mail to whoever it is you think can get you the help you need. This may be the employee assistance program at your place of work, a school counselor, clergy, trusted friend, or relative. But do it *now*. Don't wait. I wouldn't want to see you wind up like several of the respondents to a survey administered by Dr. Philip Zimbardo (page 24). In their eighties, a number of people questioned finally admitted that before they die they would like "to enjoy one non-shy day." We all deserve more than just *one* day. So please – gather up your courage and make the contact.

Whether you seek out professional assistance or not, by all means, reread <u>FACING A CROWD</u> occasionally. You will get more out of it each time you do, for when you are ready, "teachers will appear."

Final thoughts and a request

In writing this book it was my aim to assemble the proper combination of information and encouragement to assist you in reducing your anxiety and improving your public presentation skills. While sitting here tapping on my computer keys I have imagined you reading these words and benefiting from them, although I can't know for sure if either of us have met with success.

For the benefit of future readers then, I would very much appreciate hearing from you. What stories can you share about your challenges or successes with public speaking? Have you overcome your stage fright? I would love to hear about it. How has your life changed for the better? What advice would you give to others who may be living with the same fears or concerns you had for many years? What parts of this book helped you the most? Are you still experiencing some difficulties with public speaking anxiety? What sections of this book would you like to see beefed up in future editions?

By learning what has worked or not worked for you, I can provide better service in the future to others who are in need of assistance. If you would like to seize this opportunity to help fellow "tortured talkers" please share your thoughts and experiences by writing to, **Keith Clinton, c/o Drake Publishing, P.O. Box 8524, Bend, Oregon 97708-8524.** Your anonymity is absolutely guaranteed.

Thank you my friend. I wish you the very best in whatever you do. And remember—get out there and practice! KC

APPENDIX

Part I – Key Points
TO EASE YOUR ANXIETY...

Chapter 1

LEARN WHY PUBLIC SPEAKING IS AN ESSENTIAL SKILL.

1. Orators are not born—they are made.

2. Learning to speak up and say what is on your mind is a powerful skill to cultivate.

3. If we do not voice our thoughts and opinions in public settings, there are many people who will never come to know us.

4. The capacity to "stand and deliver" in front of an audience often separates those who get what they want out of life from those who do not.

Chapter 2

DISCOVER THE REASONS BEHIND THE FEAR.

1. Over 30% of the U.S. population fears public speaking more than anything else, including death.

2. 85% of all U.S. citizens experience some level of anxiety about public speaking, and only 7% say they have never experienced shyness.

3. Public speaking anxiety has several base fears including fear of: people staring, making a mistake, forgetting what to say, disappointing superiors or parents, looking foolish, being judged, and the fear of rejection.

4. The amount of anxiety we experience may be attributed to several factors including: genetics, family, cultural differences, peers, and labeling.

5. All our yesterdays shaped us into who we are today, spiritually, intellectually and emotionally. In that shaping

process (called life) some of us happened to get an extra dose of shyness or stage fright.

6. We can each make changes to who we are and how we feel about ourselves. Interestingly enough, no one else can.

Chapter 3

STUDY FAMOUS PEOPLE WHO OVERCAME INSECURITIES.

1. Most people who make their living performing still get nervous, even though they have faced countless audiences and cameras.

2. Even professionals must study and practice in order to appear natural and relaxed while delivering a seemingly effortless performance.

3. If you want something badly enough and work hard enough, you can have it.

Chapter 4

FREE YOURSELF FROM A NEGATIVE INNER VOICE.

1. Surround yourself with positive people and positive ideas. Soon, instead of seeing barriers in your way, you will see infinite possibilities.

2. Examine your life and start rejecting that which you intuitively know is bad for you.

3. Concentrate every day on being positive.

4. Once you establish a clear vision of who you want to be and what is really important to you, you will find yourself more focused, self-satisfied, and proud.

5. Focus on succeeding instead of not failing.

6. Think positive thoughts and visualize absolute success every time before going in front of an audience.

7. "Don't try, do. There is a difference between trying and doing. If you only commit to trying you have not committed to much"   ...and your fear is still in the driver's seat.

Chapter 5

PLAY THE ROLE OF A CONFIDENT PERSON, AND YOU WILL BECOME ONE.

1. Take on a different role—the role of someone who can speak confidently in front of others.

2. We are all capable of doing much more than we think we can.

3. To improve ourselves and grow we must constantly go outside of our personal comfort zone. To move from where we are to where we want to be, we must stretch ourselves and feel a little uncomfortable, a little nervous—sometimes a lot nervous.

4. There is little value in hanging back and doing only what comes easy. Get out and try new things.

5. If a person does not care about him or herself, it is unlikely anyone else will.

6. Start small and incrementally take on the traits of a confident person.

7. We cannot always control what happens to us, but we can control how we feel about it.

8. People are drawn to those who are positive and confident, like bugs to a porch light. So as you act more upbeat and confident you will acquire more friends and acquaintances.

Chapter 6

CALM YOURSELF THROUGH PROPER BREATHING.

1. Correct breathing will help settle your nerves.

2. To help yourself relax draw in a deep cleansing breath through your nose filling your lungs completely with air. Hold it for a few seconds, then exhale through your mouth. Repeat this several times.

3. When breathing properly your chest and shoulders will stay stationary while your belly swells with each inhalation.

4. By learning to breathe correctly you will be calmer and have plenty of air for speaking or any other type of vocal performance.

Chapter 7

WORK THROUGH FEAR, AND IT WILL NO LONGER CONTROL YOU.

1. Do the thing you fear and the death of fear is certain.

2. Fear will often hold us back beyond reason, keep us from enjoying life to its fullest, and stop us from accomplishing all that we are capable of.

3. Day by day, week by week, progressively put more pressure on yourself to experience ever greater challenges.

4. Through repetition and conditioned response you can train yourself to overcome the fear of public speaking just as surely as the family dog can be taught to sit for a biscuit.

5. Once you begin to deal with fear and self-doubt you will be able to seize new opportunities, to speak up, and get more of what you want out of life.

6. Worry will not change anything, so you might as well stop doing it.

Chapter 8

USE NERVOUS ENERGY TO YOUR ADVANTAGE.

1. A certain level of nervousness is not only desirable but is absolutely essential to produce an energetic public presentation.

2. At the beginning of a presentation you may feel particularly uneasy. But once you get started, this uneasiness will subside and positive energy will be left.

3. A vibrant, enthusiastic speaker is almost impossible to ignore. Nervous energy is needed to fuel this kind of performance.

4. Nervousness comes from feelings of respect and responsibility to our audience. When we care about others we want to do a good job for them.

5. Lively presentations result when nervous energy is used to produce positive thoughts, emotions, and actions.

Chapter 9

SEEK OPPORTUNITIES TO PRACTICE.

1. If you want to be good at public speaking, do it often. Push yourself to speak regularly and you will become a competent speaker.

2. When the student is ready the teacher will appear. If you are ready to learn, endless possibilities will present themselves to you.

3. For those who are serious about overcoming stage fright and improving their public speaking skills, Toastmasters International is highly recommended.

4. Meetings, work, school, parties, classes, clubs, volunteer organizations, theater and more—places for you to practice your public speaking skills are limitless. Learn to say "yes" as opportunities present themselves.

5. As you become more proficient at speaking, look for new challenges and opportunities to sharpen and maintain your skills.

6. Some people may not want you to change. But you be the judge of what is in your best interests.

Part II – *Key Points*
TO BE AN EFFECTIVE SPEAKER...

Chapter 10

GET YOURSELF READY.

1. Know your material well and know how long your presentation will take.

2. For any speech, have a firm grasp of your opening, key points, and closing.

3. Seldom will you want to memorize an entire speech. Being too scripted removes spontaneity and puts you at risk of losing your place if you forget even a single word or phrase.

4. You will always feel more nervous than you look. But no one can see your butterflies.

5. Audiences want you to succeed. They want to witness success.

6. To prepare your body for a performance, and be as physically at ease as you can be, warm up and burn off excess energy.

7. Check your appearance, then forget it. Worry gives a small thing a big shadow.

8. Concentrate on the needs of your audience, not your own needs.

9. Connect with your audience as individuals.

Chapter 11

TAKE CONTROL, USE GESTURES, AND SHOW EMOTION.

1. When introduced, nervous or not, move quickly and confidently to the front and play the role of a self-assured speaker.

2. Take control and resist the urge to think, "This is too scary."

3. Project self-assurance: people will think you have something important to say, so they will listen.

4. Lecterns and podiums are physical and psychological barriers between you and your audience. When possible, come out from behind that fortress to more closely connect with people.

5. Movement and gestures help an audience focus on the speaker. The bigger the room, the broader your movements and gestures should be.

6. Sweep the room with your eyes, frequently stopping to make direct eye contact with individuals. Connect with your listeners. Communicate with each person. Don't just talk to the back wall or a faceless crowd.

7. Project the mood and emotions that you would like your audience to experience.

8. Engage your audience and keep them involved by using a variety of participatory techniques such as asking questions, calling for a show of hands, or getting them on their feet.

Chapter 12

MAXIMIZE THE QUALITY OF YOUR VOICE.

1. Your voice is the most interesting and expressive means you have of sharing yourself with the world. It is the doorway through which people will come to know you.

2. In large spaces project your voice so that even the farthest person away can hear and understand what is being said.

3. If in doubt about whether you can be heard or understood, ask.

4. Make your presentations interesting and easier to listen to by varying your rate of delivery, pitch, and volume.

5. The more theatrical you can be with your voice, the closer people will stay focused to you and your message.

6. If you think you need to change some aspect of your voice, don't stand in the way of your own progress. Make the necessary changes and get on with expressing yourself publicly.

Chapter 13

HAVE HUMOR.

1. With humor you can break the ice, capture an audience's attention, get an audience relaxed, and put a dash of humanity into what otherwise might be a dull, factual presentation.

2. Nothing will get you on the good side of an audience quicker than humor.

3. Many speakers never try being humorous because they "can't remember any jokes." But you don't have to. That's what libraries are for.

4. Instead of just retelling jokes in their original form, tailor them to fit you and your audience.

5. Aside from classic joke telling, three other fun types of humor include twisting words and phrases around, puns, and snappy comebacks.

6. Don't walk on the laughter of your own jokes. If people aren't through laughing yet, don't interrupt them. There's no guarantee that your next joke will be as funny.

7. When beginning a story never announce, "This is the funniest thing I've ever heard." You'll raise expectations way too high and set yourself up to bomb.

8. If a story or joke does bomb, make a joke of that. A little self-deprecating humor has saved many a speaker.

9. Share your humor with the rest of the world, so we can all laugh.

Chapter 14

REPLACE BAD HABITS WITH GOOD ONES.

1. Bad habits can make a speech memorable for the wrong reasons.

2. We are usually oblivious to our own bad habits, so we need help in identifying them.

3. Ask a friend, family member, coworker, or classmate to evaluate your presentation style.

4. Annoying speech habits we unknowingly inflict upon our audiences include: filler words like "ums" and "ahs," jingling pocket change, twirling a ring, scratching, wringing our hands, flipping hair back, playing with a pen, constant throat clearing, and many more.

5. A dry throat or cough that develops *every* time you speak is a symptom of excess nervousness. Look for more opportunities to practice your public speaking skills and keep a glass of water handy.

6. *Toastmasters* clubs are an excellent place to receive routine feedback on your speaking habits, both good and bad.

Chapter 15

ACQUIRE IMPROMPTU SPEAKING SKILLS.

1. Be in the moment, listening carefully to what is going on around you.

2. Believe in yourself and seek opportunities to speak unrehearsed on the spur-of-the-moment.

3. Active listening includes focusing on the subject at hand, making eye contact with whoever has the floor, showing interest with an occasional nod, and asking questions as appropriate.

4. Form an opinion and be ready to express it.

5. Expect to be called upon.

6. Prepare mini talks you may never give.

Chapter 16

LEARN HOW TO GIVE A GOOD INTERVIEW.

1. A unique feature of print media is in-depth coverage.

2. Radio is an auditory medium. Immediacy and sound are its strengths.

3. Don't fret about microphones. They are just electronic devices to capture and amplify your voice.

4. During a television interview focus your eyes and attention on the reporter.

5. Tips for TV interviews—ignore the camera, plant your feet and don't move, clasp your hands and don't use gestures, have your key points in mind, and don't even try to use notes.

6. During any interview try to work in the answer to the question you wish you had been asked.

7. Always be ready to answer the question; "Is there anything else you would like to add?"

Part III — Key Points
TO PREPARE QUALITY PRESENTATIONS...

Chapter 17

RESEARCH WHY, WHO, WHERE, WHEN AND WHAT.

1. When asked to give a speech find out exactly what it is you are being asked to do.

2. Find out as much as you can about your audience.

3. Get the inside scoop on an audience through personal contacts, phone calls, the library, Internet and by arriving early to meet and greet people.

4. Also arrive early to become acquainted with the surroundings.

5. Know what the meeting agenda is.

6. Nothing beats old-fashioned preparation to calm your nerves. Never assume you can pull together a meaningful presentation at the last minute. For the sake of you and your audience invest the time to properly prepare.

Chapter 18

WRITE FROM THE HEART.

1. Preparing a succinct, potent speech requires planning, writing, rewriting, organizing, reorganizing and then more of the same.

2. The attention span of an audience is only as long as the seat of the pants will endure.

3. We are all more comfortable and convincing when speaking about things we know and have experienced.

Draw upon events from your own life; personalize it; and make it relevant to other people's lives.

4. Audiences want to hear interesting stories. Dry terminology and facts will seldom hold attention or convince people to take action.

5. One of the best ways to conquer writer's block is to write something—anything.

6. The mere act of doing something physical has been shown to stimulate the creative right side of the brain.

7. If short on ideas, try browsing in a library or bookstore to get your creative juices flowing.

Chapter 19

ORGANIZE YOUR INFORMATION.

1. A good story makes for a compelling speech opening. People will stop and listen.

2. After capturing your audience with an interesting opening, hang onto them with a smooth transition into the body of your speech.

3. Keep things lively to minimize mental wandering by your audience.

4. Facts and figures that are not somehow woven into an interesting tale will be easily forgotten.

5. The summation of a speech needs to wrap back around to where you started to remind listeners of the importance of your subject. A restatement of a few key points can hammer home your ideas.

6. Closing comments should be crafted to help modify audience behavior.

7. Question and Answer sessions can squeeze more valuable information out of a presentation.

8. Fearlessly face any Q&A session armed with the following few words: "I'm sorry. I don't know the answer to that, but if you'll leave your name and number I will be glad to call you with the information."

Chapter 20

MAKE EFFICIENT NOTES.

1. A minimum number of high quality notes will help you have a natural presentation style, whereas with a completely written script you will be tempted to read more, making you less effective.

2. Be selective. Pare notes down to just key words and phrases.

3. The less dependent a speaker is on notes, the freer flowing any presentation will be.

4. Hints for working with notes— Use large print. Leave plenty of white space. Highlight key words. Number cards or pages and don't staple them. Set notes down while speaking. Avoid drawing attention to your notes— as you finish with a page do not flip it over face down. Instead, simply slide the completed page or card to one side, revealing the next page below it.

Chapter 21

PLAN APPROPRIATE VISUAL AIDS.

1. Only use visual aids to *add* to a presentation. Never use them just to take the focus off of you as the presenter.

2. Visual aids should assist a speaker, not be the whole show.

3. The most common and simple visual aid is the flip chart.

4. Make sure you have the proper implements for the visual medium you plan to use.

5. When using an overhead projector, reveal only one point at a time by concealing the rest with a piece of paper. Refocus the audience's attention back to you by either turning off the projector or covering the whole transparency with a piece of paper.

6. Avoid distributing numerous handouts at one time. People will read instead of listening to you.

7. Electronic gadgets have one thing in common—the ability to not work when you flip the "on" switch. Always have a back-up plan.

8. Props can non-verbally explain objects that words alone could never do justice to. (Have you ever purchased a car sight unseen after just hearing a description of it?)

9. Be familiar with your props and practice with them before a presentation.

Part IV – Key Points
TO ACHIEVE YOUR SPEAKING GOALS...

Chapter 22

SEEK MULTIPLE SOURCES OF WISDOM.

1. To rapidly progress toward your goals, expose yourself to a variety of information and training sources.

2. Joining Toastmasters is highly recommended for you to improve your public speaking skills and overcome excess nervousness.

3. Libraries, bookstores and the Internet are good sources of information on overcoming anxieties and improving presentation skills.

4. Check with chambers of commerce, business development centers, colleges, professional societies, trade groups and your place of work for upcoming relevant seminars.

5. Private coaches can help individuals identify and solve their public speaking problems by tailoring a program to fit specific needs. Some will even help craft speeches.

6. If you have the presentation of a lifetime coming up and need help fast—seek out a private coach and commit to spending quality time on your speech.

Chapter 23

EMPLOY A FORMULA FOR SUCCESS.

1. Decide what you want.

2. Write it down.

3. Prioritize your goals.

4. List the steps needed to achieve each goal.

5. Set deadlines for yourself.

6. Do something every day toward achieving a major goal.

7. Focus on what it is you want and think about it often.

8. Consistently reach beyond what is comfortable to you. Stretch yourself.

Chapter 24

LEARN TO BELIEVE.

1. The fear of self-expression is a powerful force that holds millions of people in its grip. Many cannot escape, only because they believe they can't.

2. You can break the barriers that hold you back, but first you must believe that you can—believe in yourself.

3. Believing is seeing. As you begin to believe in success, you will see yourself being more successful.

4. While it is true that many of us are tentative and afraid to pursue our dreams, it is also true that anyone can change, take control of their life, and influence their own destiny.

5. Imagine your most perfect vision of success, then each day take another step closer to it.

Speaking Engagement Planning Sheet

Event_____

Date _____   **Time** _____

Organization_____

Meeting Place_____

Street
Address_____

Contact Person #1 _____

Phone # ___-___-____

Mailing Address

_____

E-Mail _____   FAX # ___-___-____

Pager # ___-___-____

Contact Person #2 _____

Phone # ___-___-____

Mailing Address

_____

E-Mail _____   FAX # ___-___-____

Pager # ___-___-____

Expected Attendance _____

Age (range) _____

Common Background of Audience_____

_____

Special Needs_____

_____

Props _____

Visual Aids _____

Equipment Needs_____

Handouts_____

Other Information_____

_____

_____

Copy and use.   From _FACING A CROWD – How to foil your
fear of public speaking_ © a book by Keith Clinton

SPEECH OUTLINE

Title: _____

Opening: (Grab their attention)_____
_____
_____
_____

Transition:_____
_____
_____
_____

Body:
Main Point #1_____

Support_____
_____

Main Point #2 _____

Support_____
_____

Main Point #3 _____

Support_____
_____

Conclusion: (A call to action)_____
_____
_____

SPEAKER'S CHECK LIST

(Plan ahead for a successful program.)

___ **Speech Notes**
___ **Speaking Engagement Planning Sheet**
___ **Props**
___ **Visual Aids**
___ **Overhead transparencies or Slides**
___ **Flip charts**
___ **Equipment**
___ **Projector**
___ **Screen**
___ **VCR**
___ **TV**
___ **PC**
___ **Handouts**
___ **Writing Pad**
___ **Pens/Pencils**
___ **Overhead Pens**
___ **Felt Markers**
___ **Highlighters**
___ **Pointer**
___ **Pen Light**
___ **Calendar**
___ **Phone List**
___ **Pager**
___ **Cell Phone**

Others
___
___
___
___
___

BIBLIOGRAPHY

1 **Michael T. Motley**, "Taking the Terror Out of Talk." Psychology Today, 22 January 1988.

2 **John R. Marshal, M.D.**, *Social Phobia: From Shyness to Stage Fright* (New York: Harper Collins, 1994)

3 **Jonathan Cheek, Ph.D.**, *Conquering Shyness: The Battle Anyone Can Win.* New York: G.P.Putnam's Sons, 1989:p22

4 **Philip G. Zimbardo and Shirley L. Radl**, *The Shy Child: A Parent's Guide to Overcoming and Preventing Shyness from Infancy to Adulthood*, New York: Doubleday/Dolphin, 1982: p.9, pp.17-20

5 **Burt Reynolds**, *My Life*, New York:Hyperion, 1994

6 **Howard Teichmann**, *Fonda - My Life*, New York:NAL Books, New American Library, 1981

7 **Charles Osgood**, Osgood on Speaking: *How to think on your feet without falling on your face.* New York: William Morrow and Company, Inc., 1988

8 **James Earl Jones and Penelope Niven**, *James Earl Jones - Voices and Silences*, New York: Charles Scribner's Sons, 1993

9 **Gary W. Fenchuk**, *Timeless Wisdom: Thoughts on life...the way it should be.* Midlothian, VA: Cake Eaters, Inc.,1994

10 **Norman Vincent Peale, PhD.**, *The Power of Positive Thinking*: New York: Fawcett Crest/ Ballentine Books,1952

11 **Richard Carlson**, *Don't Sweat the Small Stuff, and it's all small stuff*. New York: Hyperion, 1997

12 **Richard Hefter**, *Very Worried Walrus*, from the *Sweet Pickles Series*, Holt, Reinhart and Winston, 1977

13 **Susan Jeffers, PhD.**, *Feel The Fear And Do It Anyway: Dynamic techniques for turning fear, indecision, and anger into power, action, and love*. New York: Fawcett Columbine/ Ballentine, 1987

14 **Gene Perret and Linda Perret.**, *Gene Perret's Funny Business: Speaker's Treasury of Business Humor For All Occasions*, New Jersey: Prentice Hall, 1990

15 **Colin L. Powell** (with Joseph E. Persico), *My American Journey*. New York: Random House, 1995

16 **Dale Carnegie, Revised by Dorthy Carnegie**, *The quick and easy way to Effective Speaking:* NY,NY, Association Press, 1962

17 **Walter Anderson**, *The Confidence Course-Seven Steps To Self-Fulfillment*. New York: HarperCollins Publishers, 1997

Index

ABOUT THE AUTHOR

KEITH CLINTON set about overcoming his anxiety of facing a crowd at age 43. He diligently researched the subjects of stage fight, shyness and public speaking. Then he became an active member of Toastmasters International, joined a community theater, and took singing and voice lessons. His acquired knowledge and skills have since allowed him to inform and entertain hundreds of audiences. He was able to change his own life so dramatically, that now he is absolutely driven to help others overcome *their* fear of public expression through his writing, speaking, and private coaching.